Bible Trivia

850 Interesting Questions and Answers!

© Copyright 2024 - All rights reserved.

The content contained within this book may not be reproduced, duplicated, or transmitted without direct written permission from the author or the publisher.

Under no circumstances will any blame or legal responsibility be held against the publisher or author for any damages, reparation, or monetary loss due to the information contained within this book, either directly or indirectly.

Legal Notice:

This book is copyright-protected. It is only for personal use. You cannot amend, distribute, sell, use, quote, or paraphrase any part of the content within this book without the consent of the author or publisher.

Disclaimer Notice:

Please note the information contained within this document is for educational and entertainment purposes only. All effort has been executed to present accurate, up-to-date, reliable, and complete information. No warranties of any kind are declared or implied. Readers acknowledge that the author is not engaging in the rendering of legal, financial, medical, or professional advice. The content within this book has been derived from various sources. Please consult a licensed professional before attempting any techniques outlined in this book.

By reading this document, the reader agrees that under no circumstances is the author responsible for any losses, direct or indirect, that are incurred as a result of the use of the information contained within this document, including, but not limited to, errors, omissions, or inaccuracies.

CONTENTS

Introduction	5
Creation of the Heavens and the Earth	6
Creation of Adam and Eve	10
Garden of Eden	14
Expulsion from the Garden of Eden	18
Adam and Eve's Lineage	22
Noah and the Great Flood	28
Tower of Babel	33
Abraham and His Family	37
Isaac, Abraham's Son	44
Jacob, Esau, and Rachel	49
The Ten Plagues of Egypt	60
The Exodus	65
The Ten Commandments	70
The Journey to the Promised Land	74
Judges	77
The Kingdom of Israel and the United Monarchy	81
Goliath and David	89
Solomon and His Reign	96
Rehoboam and the Divided Kingdom	102
Elijah	107
Elisha	112
Kings of Judah and Israel	117

Prophets of the Old Testament	123
Esther and the Purim Story	134
Birth of John the Baptist	138
The Annunciation to the Blessed Virgin	142
Jesus' Birth	147
Baptism of Jesus	153
Ministry and Miracles of Jesus	159
Temptation of Jesus	168
Sermon on the Mount	172
Parables of Jesus	178
Jesus' Entry into Jerusalem	183
The Last Supper	188
Resurrection of Jesus	199
Paul's Travels	220
Disciples	229
Persecution of the Early Christians	238
Final Judgment	261
Heaven	266
Angels	272
Demons and Monsters	280
Satan	286
Conclusion	291
Answer Key	292

INTRODUCTION

Welcome to Bible Trivia: 850 Interesting Questions and Answers! Here, you will discover the answers to some of life's most interesting mysteries.

In this book, we will explore many stories found in the Bible, from the creation of the world to how heaven is depicted.

We begin with a look at how God created the heavens and earth, as well as Adam and Eve, who were placed in the Garden of Eden until their expulsion. We then move on to examine the Great Flood before delving into Abraham's family line, which includes Ishmael, Isaac, Jacob, and Esau. Answer questions about Joseph's journey home from Egypt during the ten plagues. We also take an in-depth look at Jesus' birth story, including his baptism by John the Baptist and the miracles that he performed. The final part of our book focuses on Paul's travels around Asia Minor, the early church, and the persecution of Christians. Lastly, we take a look at Jesus' Second Coming, which includes the Rapture and the Final Judgment.

By reading this book, you will gain an even greater understanding of Bible stories and how they have shaped our world. Each question is designed to help cement your knowledge of the Bible and also introduce things you may not know. All of the answers can be found at the end of the book.

We hope you enjoy!

Bible Trivia

CREATION OF THE HEAVENS AND THE EARTH

This chapter delves into God's creation as explained in Genesis. Test your knowledge by answering each multiple-choice question, which will cover topics such as when man was created, how many days it took for land and water to be separated, who said, "Let there be light," and more! Ready?

Let's get started!

1. How many days did God take to create the heavens and the earth?

a) Six
b) Seven
c) Eight
d) Nine

2. What was God's first act when creating the heavens and the earth?

a) Separation of light from darkness
b) Splitting open a great sea
c) Speaking aloud three words
d) Forming men out of the dust

3. According to the Bible, what was created on the third day of creation?

a) Animals and insects
b) Land and plants
c) Sun, moon, and stars
d) The sea

4. What is the first living creature that God created during the creation of the heavens and the earth?

a) Water and sky animals
b) Adam
c) Land animals
d) Eve

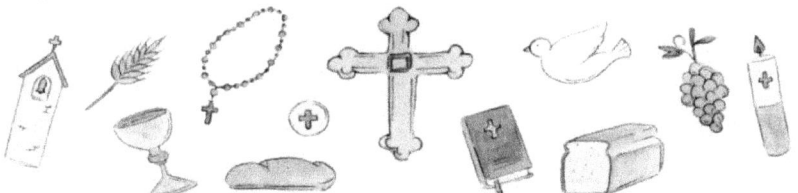

5. On which day was man created according to the Bible?

a) First day
b) Second day
c) Third day
d) Sixth day

6. Who said, "Let there be light" when creating the heavens and the earth as described in Genesis?

a) God
b) Adam
c) Noah
d) Abraham

7. According to the Bible, what did God do on the second day of creation?

a) He created the sun and moon.
b) He rested.
c) He created the sky.
d) He created man.

8. How many days did it take God to rest after creating the heavens and the earth?

a) One
b) Two
c) Three
d) Four

9. What did God do on the fourth day of creation?

a) Create the sun, moon, and stars
b) Create plants
c) Create sea creatures and birds
d) Create humans

10. According to Genesis, God saw that everything he had created was _____.

a) Ordinary
b) Good
c) Chaotic
d) Complete

Bible Trivia

CREATION OF ADAM AND EVE

This chapter delves into God's creation of humankind. Test your knowledge by answering each multiple-choice question, which will cover topics such as what kind of creature God used for creating man, why man was created according to religious tradition, and what blessing God bestowed upon them after their creation.

11. In which book of the Bible is the story of the creation of man found?

a) Exodus
b) Leviticus
c) Numbers
d) Genesis

12. According to the Bible, what did God use as his instrument to create the first man?

a) His hand
b) Dust of the ground
c) Clouds
d) The rib of Eve

13. Who was the first man mentioned in Genesis?

a) Noah
b) Abraham
c) Adam
d) Moses

14. Who was the first woman mentioned in Genesis?

a) Rebecca
b) Sarah
c) Leah
d) Eve

15. According to the Bible, what did God use to create the first woman?

a) The stars
b) The dirt
c) Breath of life
d) The rib of Adam

16. Which of the following statements about the first humans can be found in the Bible?

a) They were created in God's image.
b) They were created as equals.
c) They were made lower than animals.
d) None of these answers are correct.

17. Where did God place the first humans after creating them?

a) The Garden of Eden
b) Heaven
c) Earth
d) Mount Sinai

18. What did God give to the first humans after creating them?

a) Eternal life
b) The Garden of Eden
c) Dominion over creation
d) All of the above

19. According to religious tradition, how long did it take for God to create the first humans?

a) One day
b) Three days
c) Seven days
d) One month

20. What is said about Adam's position relative to Eve after creation?

a) Adam was not as important as Eve.
b) They were equals.
c) He was given a position of authority and leadership over her.
d) None of these answers are correct.

21. What did God command Adam and Eve to do after they were created?

a) To love each other
b) Not to eat from the tree of the knowledge of good and evil
c) To be fruitful and multiply
d) All of the above

22. Who named all of the animals according to Genesis?

a) Adam
b) Eve
c) God
d) The Serpent

Bible Trivia

GARDEN OF EDEN

These questions will test your knowledge of the Garden of Eden, the beautiful paradise where God placed Adam and Eve. This garden has captured the imagination of scholars, who have debated its location, what it looked like, and why God chose to place his beloved creations there. Let's look at some questions about the paradise God created.

23. Who was responsible for creating the Garden of Eden?
a) God
b) Adam
c) Eve
d) Satan

24. What type of tree grew at the center of the garden?
a) Palm tree
b) Cedar tree
c) Oak tree
d) Tree of the knowledge of good and evil

25. What did God forbid Adam and Eve to eat in the Garden of Eden?
a) Animals
b) Fruit from the forbidden tree
c) Vegetables
d) All of the above

26. What animal did God create to guard the entrance of the garden?
a) Wolf
b) Lion
c) Bear
d) None of the above

27. How many rivers flow out of Eden?
a) Two
b) Three
c) Four
d) Five

28. According to tradition, what color were Adam's eyes when he awoke in Eden?
a) Blue
b) Green
c) Black
d) Unknown

29. From which tree should Adam and Eve not eat?
a) Tree of the knowledge of good and evil
b) Tree of Life
c) Oak tree
d) Apple tree

30. Where does the Bible say the Garden of Eden is located?
a) Asia
b) Europe
c) Africa
d) Not specified

31. Who was told by God that they must leave the garden?

a) Adam and Eve
b) Animals
c) Angels
d) All of the above

32. In which book can we find the events that took place in Eden?

a) Genesis
b) Exodus
c) Leviticus
d) Numbers

33. What did God place in the Garden of Eden to keep Adam and Eve from reaching the Tree of Life?

a) A large river
b) Flames
c) Sea
d) Cherubim

34. What does "Eden" mean in Hebrew?

a) Place of pleasure
b) Paradise
c) Knowledge
d) Delight

Bible Trivia

EXPULSION FROM THE GARDEN OF EDEN

Humans' expulsion from the Garden of Eden is an important moment in the Bible, as it marks the moment when mankind was banished from paradise due to their disobedience. In this chapter, you will explore many questions related to this event, such as what God told Adam and Eve about the tree of the knowledge of good and evil and who tempted Adam and Eve.

35. What did God tell Adam and Eve about the tree of the knowledge of good and evil?

a) Eat from it freely.
b) Touch it as you wish.
c) Cut it down.
d) Do not eat or touch it.

36. How was sin introduced to mankind?

a) Through disobedience to God's commandment
b) By Adam killing Eve
c) Picking the wrong type of fruit
d) Refusing to worship idols

37. Who tempted Adam and Eve in the Garden of Eden?

a) A beaver
b) An angel
c) A serpent
d) No one; they were tempted by themselves.

38. According to Genesis, how does God punish the serpent?

a) He kills it.
b) He kicks it out of Eden.
c) He curses it into being forced to crawl on its belly and eat dust.
d) None of the above.

39. What did Adam and Eve wear after being expelled from the Garden of Eden?

a) Coats of skins
b) Tunics woven by angels
c) Pristine white garments
d) Nothing, they were naked

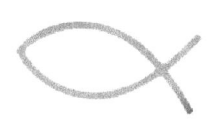

40. How long was Adam and Eve's stay in the Garden of Eden before their expulsion?

a) Unspecified
b) Three weeks
c) Forty days
d) Nine months

41. After being banished from paradise, what did God do to protect it?

a) He built an impenetrable wall around it.
b) He created fierce creatures to guard it.
c) He placed angels at its entrance.
d) He destroyed the garden.

42. What type of fruit was forbidden for Adam and Eve to eat?

a) Apple
b) Orange
c) Pear
d) Unknown

43. Why did Adam and Eve hide themselves when they heard God walking in the garden?

a) They were ashamed.
b) They wanted to play a trick on him.
c) They feared his wrath.
d) They didn't know who it was.

44. What happened after Adam and Eve ate the forbidden fruit?

a) Their eyes opened to knowledge.
b) They became mortal.
c) They were expelled from the Garden of Eden.
d) All of the above.

45. How long were Adam and Eve banished from paradise after eating the forbidden fruit?

a) Forever
b) Forty days
c) Three weeks
d) One day

46. After they were expelled, what was one thing that changed for Adam and Eve?

a) They became mortal.
b) They could no longer talk to animals.
c) They could not have any children.
d) All of the above.

Bible Trivia

ADAM AND EVE'S LINEAGE

In this section, you will explore the genealogy of Adam and Eve. Test your knowledge by answering trivia questions about their sons and daughters, grandsons and granddaughters, and so on as you make your way down their family tree. Are you ready? Let's get started!

47. How many sons did Adam and Eve have?
   a) Two
   b) Three
   c) Four
   d) Five

48. What was the name of Cain's firstborn son?
   a) Abel
   b) Enoch
   c) Seth
   d) Mahalaleel

49. Who was the son of Enoch?
   a) Noah
   b) Lamech
   c) Shem
   d) Irad

50. Who was Abraham's father?
   a) Adam
   b) Terah
   c) Noah
   d) Joshua

Bible Trivia

51. Who were the parents of Isaac?
a) Abraham and Hagar
b) Abraham and Sarah
c) Adam and Lilith
d) Jacob and Rebecca

52. What was the name of Esau's wife?
a) Rachel
b) Leah
c) Zilpah
d) Mahalath

53. What was Boaz's occupation?
a) Landowner
b) Barkeeper
c) Potter
d) Physician

54. How many named sons did David have according to the Bible?
a) One
b) Nineteen
c) Twelve
d) Fourteen

55. Who was Solomon's mother?
a) Michal
b) Jezebel
c) Bathsheba
d) Rahab

56. Who in Jesus' genealogical line had more than one wife?
a) King David
b) Rehoboam
c) Solomon
d) All of the above

57. What was the name of Jesus' earthly father?
a) Joseph
b) Jacob
c) Judah
d) Zechariah

58. Who were the parents of John the Baptist?
a) Elizabeth and Zechariah
b) Mary and Joseph
c) Ruth and Boaz
d) Sarah and Abraham

59. How many sons did Jacob have with Leah?
   a) Five
   b) Seven
   c) Six
   d) Eight

60. Who was Rachel's father?
   a) Laban
   b) Isaac
   c) Esau
   d) Reuben

61. Which biblical figure married two sisters as wives at once?
   a) Simeon
   b) Levi
   c) Jacob
   d) Judah

62. What is the name of Noah's youngest son?
   a) Shem
   b) Japheth
   c) Ham
   d) Enoch

63. What was the name of Saul's daughter?
   a) Abigail
   b) Michal
   c) Mirabel
   d) Tamar

64. Who was the father of Hezekiah?
   a) Ahaz
   b) Solomon
   c) David
   d) Rehoboam

Bible Trivia

NOAH AND THE GREAT FLOOD

Answer questions about Noah and the Great Flood! In this chapter, we will be testing your knowledge of one of the most important stories in biblical history. You'll explore questions about who was allowed into the ark and the materials used to construct it. So, dive into these trivia questions and find out just how much you know about Noah's voyage!

65. How long did it rain during the Great Flood?

a) Seven days and seven nights
b) Forty days and forty nights
c) Twenty-four hours straight
d) Thirty days and thirty nights

66. Which animals were not allowed on board with Noah?

a) Birds
b) Reptiles
c) Rodents
d) None of the above

67. Who told Noah about God's upcoming destruction?

a) Satan
b) A prophet
c) His father
d) God

68. How many animals of each species went on the ark with Noah?

a) Ten
b) Two
c) Twenty
d) Forty

69. What did God tell Noah to build the ark out of?

a) Cedar and cypress
b) Pine and oak
c) Oak and maple
d) Gopher wood

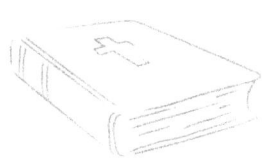

70. How many days after entering the ark did it begin to rain?

a) Five days
b) Seven days
c) Ten days
d) Fourteen days

71. Why was Noah instructed by God to bring seven pairs of some animals onto the ark?

a) To ensure that each animal had an equal chance of survival
b) To provide enough food for Noah's family during their journey
c) To sacrifice as an offering to God
d) For breeding purposes later on

72. What message from God did Noah preach before he entered the ark?

a) Repent your sins or be destroyed.
b) Turn away from evil ways.
c) Love one another.
d) None of the above.

73. What did Noah and his family do after exiting the ark?

a) Build an altar to God
b) Returned home
c) Ventured out in search of food
d) Remained on board until further instructions were given

74. Which was the first bird Noah sent out from the ark during his journey?

a) Dove
b) Raven
c) Parakeet
d) Robin

75. Which mountain peak did the ark eventually land on?

a) Mount Ararat
b) Mount Everest
c) Mount Sinai
d) Mount Olympus

76. What did Noah do after the floodwaters receded?

a) Traveled the world
b) Became a farmer
c) Became a shipbuilder
d) Unspecified

77. When was the event known as the Great Flood believed by some scholars to have taken place?

a) 5000 BCE
b) 8000 BCE
c) 10,500 BCE
d) 12,000 BCE

78. What did God promise Noah after the flood?

a) To never send such punishment again
b) To give him and his family riches
c) That he would be remembered forever
d) All of the above

79. Who else was allowed to enter the ark with Noah?

a) Family members
b) Foreigners
c) Friends from their village
d) Servants he hired for the journey

TOWER OF BABEL

The Tower of Babel is a story of great ambition and failure. In this section, we'll explore questions about what happened with the Tower of Babel, as well as its purpose and consequences. Let's dig deeper into this famous biblical tale and find out some fascinating trivia!

80. Where was the Tower of Babel located according to the Bible?

a) Athens
b) Jerusalem
c) Shinar
d) Rome

81. What was the purpose of building the Tower of Babel?

a) To create a city with many languages and cultures
b) To build an astronomical observatory to observe stars and planets in the sky
c) To make a name for themselves by reaching heaven
d) To worship God from atop a tall tower

82. According to the Bible, who initiated the construction of the Tower of Babel?

a) Nimrod
b) Noah
c) Abraham
d) None of the above

83. What was the result of building the Tower of Babel?

a) God confused people's language so they spoke different languages.
b) The builders reached heaven.
c) All the people adopted one language.
d) People became wealthier.

84. Which language were people speaking before they attempted to build the Tower of Babel?

a) English
b) Hebrew
c) Babylonian
d) Unspecified.

85. What did God think of the Tower of Babel?

a) He liked it.
b) He found it amusing.
c) He disapproved.
d) He was indifferent.

86. Who scattered the people who were working on the Tower of Babel?

a) The pharaoh
b) Nimrod
c) Moses
d) God

87. Which book in the Bible mentions the Tower of Babel?

a) Exodus
b) Genesis
c) Numbers
d) Psalms

Bible Trivia

88. What did God do when he saw how high they had built the tower?
a) He praised them.
b) He destroyed it.
c) He protected them.
d) He intervened to stop them.

89. Who said, "Come, let us go down and there confuse their language?"
a) The pharaoh
b) An angel
c) Moses
d) God

ABRAHAM AND HIS FAMILY

Answer questions about the amazing story of Abraham and his family. From Abraham's calling to the incredible faithfulness of Sarah, this section is full of fascinating trivia questions that will test your knowledge.

90. What was Abraham's profession before following God?
a) Shepherd
b) Carpenter
c) Stonecutter
d) It's not mentioned.

91. Who was the mother of Ishmael, Abraham's firstborn son?
a) Sarah
b) Hagar
c) Rachel
d) Leah

92. How many sons were born to Sarah and Abraham in Genesis?
a) One
b) Two
c) None
d) Three

93. What did Abraham tell Isaac before sacrificing him to God?
a) "God will provide the lamb for his own sacrifice."
b) "You are my only son, and I love you very much."
c) "Do not be afraid; I am here with you."
d) "Let us make a covenant with God."

94. What did Sarah tell Abraham to do with Hagar and Ishmael?

a) Kill them both.
b) Let them stay.
c) Send them away.
d) Offer up Ishmael as a sacrifice to God.

95. Which of these was the covenant that God made with Abraham?

a) A promise not to act wickedly again
b) That he would be Abraham's shield and protector
c) That he would make him the father of many sons
d) That he would earn great riches

96. What is the significance of Melchizedek?

a) He was an angel sent by God to bless Abraham.
b) He provided bread and wine as gifts for Abraham.
c) He gave bread and wine as offerings to God.
d) He was king at the time Abraham returned from battle victorious.

97. How old was Sarah when she gave birth to Isaac?

a) Seventy-five years old
b) Sixty-five years old
c) Ninety years old
d) Twenty years old

98. Who suggested giving the maidservant Hagar to Abraham so that he could have a child with her?

a) God
b) The pharaoh
c) The servant
d) Sarah

99. Where did Abraham and his family move after leaving Haran?

a) Egypt
b) Israel
c) Canaan
d) Ur

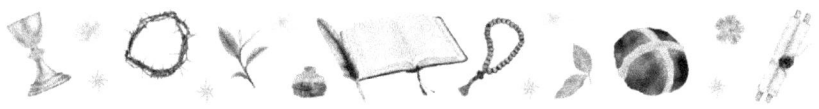

100. What does the name "Sarah" mean in Hebrew?

a) Beauty
b) Daughter
c) Princess of nations
d) Blessing from God

101. How did Sarah respond to God's promise of a son?

a) She was overjoyed.
b) She laughed in disbelief.
c) She wept.
d) She remained silent.

102. What did the pharaoh give Abraham and Sarah because Sarah was so beautiful?

a) Servants
b) Livestock
c) All of the above
d) None of the above

103. How old was Abraham when he departed for Canaan?

a) Fifty years old
b) Forty years old
c) Thirty years old
d) Seventy-five years old

104. Where did Sarah die?

a) Bethlehem
b) Canaan
c) Egypt
d) Beersheba

105. What nation did Ishmael become the ancestor of?

a) Jews
b) Egyptians
c) Assyrians
d) Arabs

106. What was Ishmael's mother's occupation?

a) A slave from Egypt
b) A farmer
c) An angel
d) A Canaanite woman

107. How old was Abraham when he had Ishmael?

a) 75 years old
b) 85 years old
c) 95 years old
d) 105 years old

108. Where did Ishmael's mother live after she left with her son?

a) Egypt
b) The wilderness of Paran
c) Gilead
d) Canaan

109. How many sons did Ishmael have when he died?

a) Twelve sons
b) Zero sons
c) Fourteen sons
d) Seven sons

110. Who told Ishmael's mother where to find water for herself and her baby while they were wandering in the desert?
a) *An angel*
b) *Sarah*
c) *Abraham*
d) *God*

Bible Trivia

ISAAC, ABRAHAM'S SON

In this chapter, we will explore the biblical stories involving Isaac. You'll be tested on your knowledge of these amazing tales, from what offering was presented when Abraham dedicated his son to how many camels were sent back with Rebecca's servant. Let us begin our journey into understanding more about the birth of one of God's most beloved sons.

111. With whom had Abraham agreed on the land on which Isaac's birthplace would be?
a) Abimelech
b) Isaac
c) Esau
d) Jacob

112. Where was the place Abraham almost sacrificed his son?
a) Moriah
b) Jehovah Jireh
c) Beersheba
d) Hebron

113. Who was instructed by God to take Isaac on a journey?
a) Sarah
b) Hagar
c) Ishmael
d) Abraham

114. What does "Isaac" mean?
a) Joyful laughter
b) One who is chosen by God
c) The one who will be great
d) Virtuous man

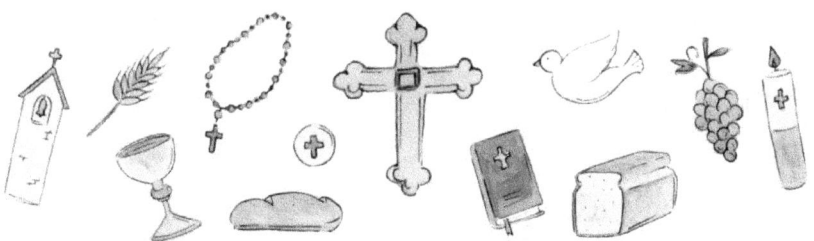

115. Who was sent with Abraham and Issac on their journey?

a) Angels
b) Servants
c) Animals
d) No one

116. Who married Isaac?

a) Rebecca
b) Sarah
c) Esther
d) None of the above

117. How many camels did Abraham send back with a servant to fetch Rebecca?

a) Five camels
b) Ten camels
c) Fifteen camels
d) Twenty camels

118. Who was sent by God to warn Abimelech and keep his hand from harming Isaac?

a) An angel
b) A prophet
c) God appeared in a dream.
d) A servant

119. How old was Abraham when he had Isaac?

a) One hundred years old
b) Eighty years old
c) Sixty years old
d) Forty years old

120. What kind of burial plot did Isaac purchase for his father Abraham after his death?

a) A cave in the wilderness of Machpelah
b) A field near Bethel
c) The Garden of Eden
d) Gilead

121. What animal was provided by God as a substitute sacrifice for Isaac?

a) Goat
b) Sheep
c) Ram
d) Cow

122. What did an angel tell Abraham before he provided the substitute sacrifice for Isaac?

a) "Do not lay a hand on the boy."
b) "Take your son, your only son."
c) "I will provide a lamb for you."
d) "This is my beloved son in whom I am well pleased."

Bible Trivia

123. What did God say after he saw that Abraham had faith in his instructions regarding sacrificing Isaac?
   a) "You have done what is right in My sight."
   b) "You have proved your faithfulness to Me."
   c) "I am greatly pleased with you."
   d) "Now I know that you fear God."

124. What does the story of the sacrifice of Isaac signify in terms of religious beliefs?
   a) The power and glory of God
   b) The strength in family ties
   c) Obedience toward authority figures
   d) Reverence for life, even animals

125. How many days did it take Abraham and Isaac to reach the mountain?
   a) Three days
   b) Seven days
   c) Ten days
   d) Fourteen days

126. According to the Bible, where was Abraham when he received the command to sacrifice his son?
   a) Shechem
   b) Hebron
   c) Rome
   d) Salem

JACOB, ESAU, AND RACHEL

Experience the epic saga of Jacob, Esau, and Rachel in this section. Through these questions, you will learn about their struggles and triumphs as they attempt to fulfill a divine prophecy that would shape events for millennia. See if you can answer each question correctly!

127. According to the Bible, what did Esau sell his birthright for?
   a) A bowl of stew
   b) Money and goods from Laban's house
   c) The firstborn lamb in Jacob's flock
   d) Gold coins from Abraham's treasure trove

128. What was the name of Isaac and Rebecca's second son?
   a) Levi
   b) Ruben
   c) Jacob
   d) Esau

129. Who told Rebecca that she would give birth to two sons who would be rivals?
   a) Gabriel
   b) Peter
   c) Moses
   d) God

130. Why was it so important for Jacob to receive his father's blessing?
   a) To bless his children
   b) To receive the family inheritance
   c) To have a higher standing in the community
   d) To protect him from Esau's wrath

131. What did Rebecca do so that Jacob could get his father's blessing?

a) She lied to Isaac about who was asking for the blessing.
b) She asked God for help.
c) She prayed fervently.
d) She tricked Esau into leaving.

132. What did Jacob dream about?

a) How far he had come on his journey
b) Angels ascending and descending a ladder
c) Future events
d) Abraham taking his son to be sacrificed

133. How many years did Jacob work for Laban before he married Rachel?

a) Seven years
b) Ten years
c) Fourteen years
d) Twenty years

134. Who tricked Isaac into giving Jacob the blessing instead of Esau?

a) Rebecca and Jacob
b) Leah
c) Esau
d) Jacob

135. What did Esau do when he realized that Jacob had tricked him out of his blessing?
a) He threatened to kill Jacob.
b) He wept bitterly.
c) He begged for Isaac's forgiveness.
d) He cursed God and renounced his name.

136. How did Rebecca try to protect Jacob from Esau's anger?
a) She advised him to flee to Laban.
b) She prayed hard for his protection against Esau's wrath.
c) She gave him weapons to protect himself.
d) She told the village about Esau's wrath.

137. How many wives did Jacob have during his life?
a) One wife
b) Two wives
c) Three wives
d) Four wives

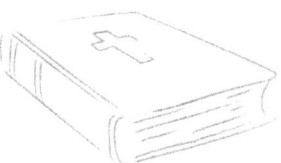

138. How did Rachel respond when her father asked who had stolen his idols?
a) She denied it.
b) She confessed that she had taken them.
c) She pleaded with him for forgiveness.
d) She offered to pay him back in some way.

139. Where did Jacob die?

a) Egypt
b) Haran
c) Mount Moriah
d) Beersheba

140. What did Jacob's twelve sons go on to become?

a) Acrobats
b) The fathers of the twelve tribes of Israel
c) Wealthy landowners
d) Teachers

Bible Trivia

JOSEPH AND HIS JOURNEY

Joseph's journey is a story of faith, resilience, courage, and divine guidance. In this section, we will explore questions about pivotal moments that molded Joseph's destiny, such as what led him to be sold into slavery.

141. What is Joseph's father's name?
a) Jacob
b) Judah
c) Abraham
d) Isaac

142. Why did Joseph's brothers sell him into slavery?
a) They were disgusted that Joseph didn't bathe.
b) They were jealous of Joseph.
c) They were tired of hearing Joseph complain.
d) They were bored.

143. What did the brothers do to Joseph before selling him into slavery?
a) Threw him in a cistern
b) Stole his beautiful robe
c) Both A and B
d) None of the above

144. How old was Joseph when he became the pharaoh's right-hand man?
a) Sixteen years old
b) Twenty years old
c) Thirty years old
d) Forty years old

145. In which country does most of Joseph's story take place?
a) Egypt
b) Israel
c) Greece
d) Italy

146. How many sons did Joseph have during his time in Egypt?
a) One
b) Two
c) Three
d) Four

147. What did Joseph's brothers do to get food during the famine?
a) Traded garments
b) Sold another brother into slavery
c) Traveled to Egypt
d) Grew enough crops in the fields

148. To whom did the pharaoh give the task of collecting and storing grain during the seven years of plenty?
a) Jacob
b) The Israelites
c) Potiphar
d) Joseph

149. Who convinced the pharaoh that it was God who had given Joseph his dream interpretation skills?
   a) His wife
   b) The magicians
   c) His advisors
   d) Joseph himself

150. How many dreams did the pharaoh have before meeting with Joseph about them?
   a) One
   b) Two
   c) Three
   d) Four

151. What was the name of Joseph's first son?
   a) Manasseh
   b) Ephraim
   c) Benjamin
   d) Reuben

152. Where did Joseph keep the grain he collected during the seven years of plenty?
   a) In cisterns in different Egyptian cities
   b) At the pharaoh's palace
   c) In his own storage bins
   d) On ships in the Nile River

153. How many brothers did Joseph have?
a) Five
b) Six
c) Seven
d) Eleven

154. With whom did Jacob reunite after twenty-two years?
a) Joseph
b) Judah
c) Benjamin
d) Isaac

155. What was the name of Joseph's youngest son born in Egypt?
a) Reuben
b) Benjamin
c) Naphtali
d) Ephraim

Bible Trivia

THE TEN PLAGUES OF EGYPT

The Ten Plagues of Egypt is a memorable event in the Bible. What was the first plague? How many days did the plague of darkness last? And who was spared from the plagues? These questions and more await you in this section!

156. What was the first plague that God sent upon Egypt?
a) Locusts
b) Darkness
c) Blood in the Nile River
d) Frogs

157. How many days did the plague of darkness last?
a) Three days
b) Five days
c) Seven days
d) Ten days

158. What was the third plague?
a) Frogs
b) Gnats or lice
c) Death of firstborns
d) None of the above

159. What animal is mentioned as part of the fifth plague in Egypt?
a) Wolf
b) Chicken
c) Horse
d) Cattle

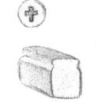     

160. Who was spared from most of the plagues?

a) The Israelites
b) The pharaoh and his court
c) The Egyptians
d) All of the above

161. What was the ninth plague that God sent upon Egypt?

a) Locusts
b) Boils
c) Hail
d) Darkness

162. Which one of these things is not mentioned as being affected by hail in Exodus?

a) People
b) Animals
c) Trees
d) None of the above

163. What was the nature of the tenth plague?

a) Devastation of the countryside
b) Death of sheep and cattle
c) Rain of fire
d) Death of all Egyptian firstborns

164. Who spoke to Moses when giving him instructions for the ten plagues of Egypt?

a) Nobody
b) God
c) A cloud
d) The pharaoh's daughter

165. Jews remember the exodus of Israelites from Egypt with which event?

a) Yom Kippur
b) Passover
c) Shavuot
d) Sukkot

166. Who does the pharaoh instruct to be spared from his command to kill all Hebrew newborns?

a) The newborn Hebrew daughters
b) His firstborn son
c) Newborns born to wealthy families
d) None of the above

167. What happened when Moses stretched out his staff over Egypt during the plague of locusts?

a) The locusts appeared.
b) God sent an angel down.
c) God caused the wind to blow.
d) There were heavy rains.

168. What animal was used as a sacrifice by the Israelites during the tenth plague?

a) A lamb
b) A goat
c) An ox
d) An eagle

THE EXODUS

The Exodus tells the story of Moses and the Israelites' miraculous journey out of slavery in Egypt. Who said, "Let my people go?" What happened to the pharaoh when he followed the Israelites into the Red Sea? Discover many more trivia questions about this important biblical event.

Bible Trivia

169. What was the name of Moses' brother?
a) Aaron
b) Isaac
c) Jacob
d) Joseph

170. How did the pharaoh die?
a) Killed in battle by the Israelites
b) In an accident while traveling with his family to a new kingdom
c) By drowning in the Red Sea after God parted it for Moses and his people
d) From old age after living a long life

171. Who said, "Let my people go?"
a) God
b) Pharaoh
c) Aaron
d) Moses

172. Who led the Israelites out of Egypt?
a) God
b) Aaron
c) Joshua
d) Moses

173. When did God promise Moses that he would deliver his people from slavery in Egypt?
a) After the ten plagues were inflicted upon the pharaoh
b) After the burning bush experience
c) Before Moses was born
d) In a dream

174. Who is believed to be the pharaoh's daughter who found and raised Moses as her own son?
a) Asenath
b) Zipporah
c) Miriam
d) Bithiah

175. How long did the Israelites wander in the wilderness until they reached Mount Sinai?
a) Forty years
b) Ten years
c) Three days
d) Seven years

176. What miracle did God perform during the Exodus that enabled the Israelites to cross through the Red Sea on dry land?
a) He made it flood with water.
b) He instructed Moses to divide it.
c) He gave them wings to fly over.
d) He stopped its flow and hardened its bottom.

177. About how old was Moses when he led his people out of Egypt?

a) Eighty years old
b) Thirty years old
c) Forty years old
d) Seventy years old

178. How many men were taken out of Egypt during the Exodus?

a) 600,000
b) 6 million
c) 60 million
d) 1 million

179. Who brought water from the rock when the children of Israel thirsted in the desert?

a) Joshua
b) Aaron
c) Miriam
d) Moses

180. What did God provide for the Israelites to eat during their journey in the desert?

a) Manna and quail
b) Fish and bread
c) Olives and fruit
d) Cattle and sheep

181. How did God guide the Israelites while they were in the wilderness?

a) A pillar of smoke
b) A pillar of cloud and a pillar of fire
c) He gave them a map.
d) He sent birds to guide the way.

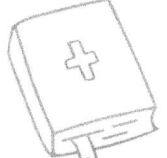

182. What did the Israelites construct to worship while Moses was on Mount Sinai?

a) A silver bull
b) An altar
c) A golden calf
d) Nothing

THE TEN COMMANDMENTS

Explore the biblical origins of a set of laws that shaped cultures around the world: the Ten Commandments. Explore questions about this legendary set of laws, such as who wrote them down and what they say. Get ready as we take you on a journey back in time to trace some of mankind's earliest attempts at moral order.

183. Who wrote the Ten Commandments?
a) Moses
b) Aaron
c) Joshua
d) Abraham

184. On what were the Ten Commandments written?
a) Stone tablets
b) Parchment paper
c) A cave wall
d) Papyrus scrolls

185. What mountain did God appear on when he gave the Ten Commandments to Moses?
a) Mount Sinai
b) Zion Hill
c) Ararat Mountain
d) Olivet Mount

186. How many of the Ten Commandments are related to worshiping other gods?
a) Two
b) Five
c) Six
d) Eight

187. Which of the following is not one of the Ten Commandments?

a) Honor your father and mother.
b) Do not murder.
c) Do unto others as you would have them do unto you.
d) Worship no other gods.

188. What is the central theme of the Ten Commandments?

a) Stay loyal to God
b) Be a lawful citizen
c) Make sure that children get a good religious education
d) None of the above

189. Which of the following sins are forbidden by the Ten Commandments?

a) Stealing
b) Killing
c) Adultery
d) All of the above

190. Which of these is not mentioned in the Ten Commandments?

a) Loving your neighbors
b) Building altars to God
c) Honoring your father and mother
d) None of the above

191. What does Exodus mean when it says, "You shall not bear false witness against thy neighbor?"

a) Do not tell lies about others.

b) Do unto others as you would have them do unto you.

c) Honor your father and mother.

d) Always support your neighbor.

Bible Trivia

THE JOURNEY TO THE PROMISED LAND

The journey to the Promised Land is a fascinating story full of adventures and challenges. It was an incredible feat, but who even led it? That is just one of the questions we will be exploring as we delve into this epic part of the Bible. So, buckle your seatbelts, and let's get started!

192. Who led the Israelites to the Promised Land?
a) Moses
b) Aaron
c) Elijah
d) Joshua

193. How many spies were sent by Moses to explore Canaan before entering it?
a) Four
b) Six
c) Twelve
d) Fourteen

194. How many tribes were there in the Promised Land at the time of entry by the Israelites?
a) Twelve tribes
b) Thirteen tribes
c) Fourteen tribes
d) Fifteen tribes

195. What river did the Israelites cross to enter the Promised Land?
a) The Nile River
b) The Jordan River
c) The Seine River
d) The Euphrates River

196. What was the first city conquered by the Israelites after crossing the Jordan River?
a) Ai
b) Babylon
c) Jericho
d) Bethlehem

197. How many times did they circle Jericho during their march around it before breaking down its walls?
a) Seven days
b) Three days
c) Five days
d) Nine days

JUDGES

As we follow the story of the Israelites' journey from Egypt to the Promised Land, some of the central characters are a series of judges. These judges were appointed by God, and their task was to lead and protect his people during their most difficult times. Test your knowledge about the judges with this chapter.

198. Who is the last judge mentioned in the Book of Judges?
a) Samuel
b) Gideon
c) Jair
d) Othniel

199. How did Ehud kill King Eglon of Moab?
a) He attacked him with a knife hidden under his cloak.
b) He stabbed him with a spear while he was sleeping.
c) He strangled him during a wrestling match.
d) He tricked him into drinking poisoned wine.

200. Why did Abimelech destroy the city of Shechem?
a) He wanted to punish its people for not supporting him.
b) He was ordered by God.
c) The people insulted his mother.
d) He wanted more land and resources.

201. What did Jephthah promise if he defeated the Ammonites?
a) A fifth of all his possessions
b) One hundred sheep
c) All the gold from the temples
d) To sacrifice whatever came out first when he returned home

202. What is unique about Ibzan's family?
a) They were descended from Joshua.
b) They had sixty sons and daughters.
c) They owned three hundred donkeys.
d) All seven of his wives were sisters.

203. Who do Gideon and his three hundred soldiers fight against?
a) Egyptians
b) Philistines
c) Ammonites
d) Midianites

204. What was unique about Shamgar's weapon?
a) It was an oxgoad.
b) It had two blades.
c) It never needed sharpening.
d) It weighed more than fifty pounds.

205. What title does Deborah have in the Book of Judges?
a) Prophet
b) Mother
c) Queen
d) Warrior

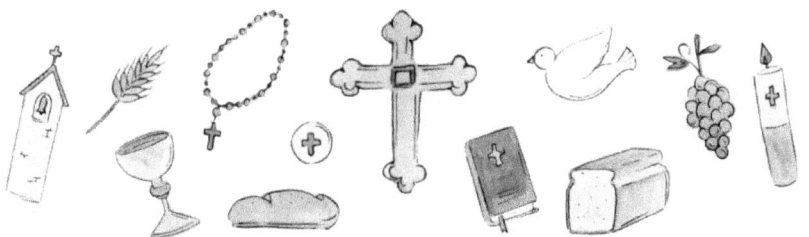

206. How does God help Gideon defeat his enemy?

a) He sends an angel to give him courage.

b) He makes his army larger.

c) He plagues the enemy with frogs.

d) He turns their swords against each other.

207. Who helped Abimelech become king of Shechem?

a) The people of Israel

b) God

c) The Philistines

d) His family

208. What happened to Samson in Gaza?

a) He was greeted in a friendly manner by the locals.

b) He was seized by the Philistines.

c) He became their judge.

d) None of the above.

209. Who is credited with killing one thousand men in one day?

a) Samson

b) Gideon

c) Abimelech

d) Shamgar

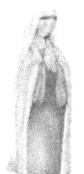    

THE KINGDOM OF ISRAEL AND THE UNITED MONARCHY

In this section, we will explore some exciting questions about one of the most influential periods in Jewish history. Who was King Solomon's father? Who wrote the Book of Proverbs in the Bible? Let us journey together to uncover these answers!

210. Who was King Solomon's father?
 a) Saul
 b) David
 c) Jacob
 d) Joseph

211. Who was the first king of Israel?
 a) Saul
 b) David
 c) Solomon
 d) Abraham

212. When did David become king of Israel?
 a) 9th century BCE
 b) 5th century BCE
 c) 11th century BCE
 d) 12th century BCE

213. Who is the author of the Book of Proverbs in the Bible?
 a) Solomon
 b) Moses
 c) Abraham
 d) Isaiah

214. How many years did it take King Solomon to build his temple?
   a) Ten
   b) Two
   c) Twenty
   d) Seven

215. Who was responsible for rebuilding Jerusalem's walls after they were destroyed by Nebuchadnezzar?
   a) Nehemiah
   b) Isaiah
   c) David
   d) Elijah

216. What is the name of King David's son who succeeded him as king?
   a) Absalom
   b) Solomon
   c) Hezekiah
   d) Adonijah

217. Who was the first judge in Israel?
   a) Gideon
   b) Othniel
   c) Deborah
   d) Samson

218. With whom did David have to compete to succeed to the throne after the death of Saul?
a) Jonathan
b) David is
c) Solomon
d) Ish-bosheth

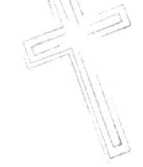

219. Who was Saul's father before he became king?
a) Abner
b) Ish-bosheth
c) Kish
d) Boaz

220. Who is the author of the Book of Ecclesiastes in the Bible?
a) Solomon
b) Moses
c) David
d) Isaiah

221. Who among these was not the king of a united Israel?
a) Saul
b) David
c) Solomon
d) Jeroboam

222. How many years did the United Monarchy last?

a) 120 years
b) 200 years
c) 300 years
d) 400 years

223. Which prophet anointed King Saul as ruler over all of Israel?
a) Elijah
b) Elisha
c) Samuel
d) Isaiah

224. Which king of Israel built a palace in Jerusalem?

a) Saul
b) Solomon
c) David
d) None of the above

225. Which books in the Bible are concerned with the reign of King David?
a) Revelation
b) Samuel
c) Kings
d) Leviticus

226. In which battle did King Saul die?
a) Battle of Mount Gilboa
b) Battle of Jericho
c) Battle of Gath
d) Battle of Hebron

227. Which of King David's sons attempted to overthrow his father?
a) Solomon
b) Rehoboam
c) Absalom
d) Hezekiah

228. What is the name of the religious book that talks about Saul's reign?
a) Judges
b) Psalms
c) The Song of Songs
d) None of the above

229. Which of the following cities did Solomon rebuild during his reign?
a) Jericho
b) Hazor
c) Jaffa
d) Kamon

230. What type of weapon did Saul throw at David?
a) Spear
b) Sword
c) Bow and arrow
d) Mace

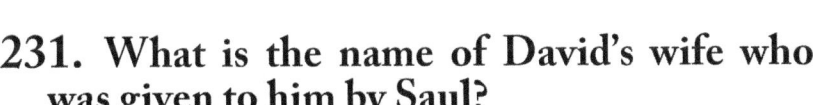

231. What is the name of David's wife who was given to him by Saul?
a) Michal
b) Abigail
c) Bathsheba
d) Ruth

232. Where did David defeat Goliath?
a) Jericho
b) Mount Olive
c) Valley of Elah
d) Gath

233. Who succeeded Solomon and became king after him?
a) Rehoboam
b) Hezekiah
c) Absalom
d) Ahaziah

234. How many wives did King Solomon have according to the Bible?

a) Three hundred wives
b) Five hundred wives
c) Seven hundred wives
d) Nine hundred wives

235. Who was the last king of a united Israel?

a) David
b) Solomon
c) Jeroboam
d) Hezekiah

236. How many years did Saul reign over Israel?

a) Twenty years
b) Thirty years
c) Forty years
d) Fifty years

237. David had two capitals. One of them was Jerusalem. What was his other capital?

a) Jericho
b) Hebron
c) Nazareth
d) Bethlehem

GOLIATH AND DAVID

Now, we will dive into some of Israel's more famous stories and reigns. In this chapter, we will explore the epic battle between Goliath and David. Answer questions about the characters who were involved and the circumstances that led to one of the Bible's most well-known moments.

238. What was the name of Goliath's brother?
a) Abner
b) Shammah
c) Lahminia
d) Saph

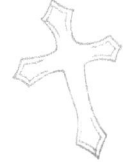

239. How many brothers did David have?
a) Four
b) Seven
c) Ten
d) Twelve

240. What weapon did David use to kill Goliath?
a) Mace
b) Spear
c) Bow and arrow
d) Slingshot

241. Which book in the Bible can you find the story about David and Goliath?
a) Psalms
b) Judges
c) Samuel

d) Kings

242. How tall was Goliath according to the Bible?
a) A little more than six cubits
b) Over six feet tall
c) Exactly nine feet
d) Seven cubits and a half

243. Who did Goliath fight for?
a) The Babylonians
b) The Egyptians
c) The Philistines
d) None of the above

244. When David killed Goliath, what did he do with his head?
a) He buried it.
b) He brought it to Jerusalem.
c) He hung it from a wall.
d) He threw it into the sea.

245. How old was David when he fought Goliath?
a) Fifteen
b) Twenty
c) Thirty
d) Not stated

246. What did King Saul promise to give to whoever killed Goliath?
a) A crown
b) A palace
c) A robe
d) His daughter

247. What did David wear when he fought Goliath?
a) Heavy metal armor
b) Bronze chainmail
c) Leather armor
d) His everyday clothes

248. Where were David's parents living at the time that Samuel anointed him as king over Israel?
a) Bethel
b) Bethlehem
c) Hebron
d) Mizpah

249. What did David do with the sword of Goliath?
a) He threw it away.
b) He kept it.
c) He gave it to Samuel.

d) He melted it down and made another one.

250. What was David's occupation?
a) Shepherd
b) Merchant
c) Miner
d) None of the above

251. Which instrument is David said to have played?
a) Lute
b) Lyre
c) Harp
d) None of the above

252. How many days did the battle between David and Goliath last?
a) One day
b) Three days
c) Seven days
d) Ten days

253. What did David bring to his brothers who were serving in the Israelite army when he first arrived at the battlefield?
a) Weapons
b) News from Saul
c) Clothing
d) Food

254. How many stones did David take with him when he went out to fight Goliath?

a) One
b) Three
c) Five
d) Seven

255. What did Saul give David to help him fight Goliath?

a) The best sword in the land
b) His armor
c) A potion of healing
d) None of the above

Bible Trivia

SOLOMON AND HIS REIGN

Solomon was known for his wisdom and wealth. He is credited with several accomplishments that made him one of Israel's greatest kings. Answer questions about Solomon's family and his rule, such as Solomon's famous judgment over a baby. Join us now on our journey through the reign of Solomon!

256. What was the name of David's first son born to Bathsheba?
a) Nathan
b) Rehoboam
c) Amnon
d) Solomon

257. How old was King David when he died in Jerusalem, making way for Solomon to become king?
a) Seventy years old
b) Thirty years old
c) Eighty years old
d) Forty years old

258. What did Solomon rule in the famous judgment over a baby?
a) The baby should be given up for adoption.
b) The baby should be split in half.
c) The baby should die.
d) The baby should remain at the palace.

259. What happened to the baby in that judgment?
a) It was split in half.
b) It went home with its rightful mother.
c) It stayed at the palace with Solomon.
d) None of the above.

260. Who helped Solomon build the First Temple in Jerusalem?

   a) Moses
   b) Hiram
   c) David
   d) Abraham

261. What did the Queen of Sheba give to King Solomon as a gift when she visited him?
   a) Gold
   b) Jewels
   c) Spices
   d) All of the above

262. What does the Bible say that made God so angry with Solomon that he took away most of his kingdom after his death?
   a) He worshiped other gods.
   b) He neglected his people.
   c) He ignored prophetic warnings.
   d) He refused to build temples in Jerusalem.

263. Which prophet warned King Solomon not to marry foreign women or worship their false gods?
   a) Elijah
   b) Elisha
   c) Isaiah
   d) Ahijah

264. What did Solomon build first in Jerusalem?
a) The Temple
b) The palace
c) The wall
d) Houses

265. How many years did King Solomon reign?
a) Twenty years
b) Forty years
c) Ten years
d) Thirty years

266. What kind of labor was forced upon the people during the time of King Solomon's rule?
a) Military service
b) Agricultural labor
c) Building projects
d) All of the above

267. According to tradition, who wrote Song of Songs?
a) David
b) Moses
c) Isaiah
d) Solomon

268. Who led an army against Jerusalem when they refused to pay taxes imposed by King Solomon?
a) The Egyptians
b) The Ammonites
c) The Philistines
d) None of the above

269. What year is it believed that construction on the temple began?
a) 967 BCE
b) 1000 BCE
c) 837 BCE
d) 722 BCE

270. Which queen came to visit Solomon during his reign?
a) The queen of Egypt
b) The queen of the Philistines
c) The queen of Sheba
d) None of the above

271. What is recorded as being one of the greatest attributes of King Solomon?
a) His wisdom
b) His vow of poverty
c) His strength
d) His vow of chastity

272. What is the name that was given to Solomon's Temple after it was rebuilt in 516 BCE?

a) Solomon's Temple
b) The Jerusalem Temple
c) The Second Temple
d) Solomon's Palace

273. What did King Solomon request from God to rule his kingdom justly and wisely?

a) Riches
b) Strength
c) Power
d) Wisdom

Bible Trivia

REHOBOAM AND THE DIVIDED KINGDOM

This chapter looks at the events that followed Rehoboam's ascension to the throne of Judah after his father's death. It explains how he angered the people of Israel. Many interesting facts about this period will be revealed in this chapter. Get ready to explore Rehoboam and the divided kingdom!

274. What did Rehoboam do to anger the people of Israel and cause them to rebel against him?
   a) Refused their request for lighter taxes
   b) Started worshiping idols
   c) Appointed wicked rulers
   d) Allied with Egypt

275. What name did Jeroboam give his new kingdom after he rebelled from Rehoboam?
   a) Judah
   b) Benjamin
   c) Ephraim
   d) Israel

276. Who intervened to stop a conflict between Jeroboam and Rehoboam from breaking out?
   a) Shemaiah
   b) Samuel
   c) David
   d) Nathan

277. Who was the first king of Israel after it split from Judah?
   a) Jeroboam
   b) Ahaziah
   c) Solomon
   d) Rehoboam

278. What did Jeroboam set up to lead people away from worshiping God in Jerusalem?
a) False prophets
b) Idols
c) Temples
d) Altars

279. Who told Rehoboam to listen to what the people wanted and reduce their burden?
a) Nathan
b) Elijah
c) Samuel
d) The elders

280. Who was the king of Judah after Rehoboam died?
a) Abijah
b) Asa
c) Azariah
d) Jedidiah

281. Who was the son of Rehoboam?
a) Abijah
b) Asa
c) Azariah
d) Jeroboam

282. How long did Jeroboam reign over Israel?

a) Two years
b) Ten years
c) A little over twenty years
d) Forty years

283. How many tribes were there in total in both kingdoms after they were divided?

a) Five
b) Six
c) Ten
d) Twelve

284. Who was the king of Judah after Abijah died?

a) Asa
b) Azariah
c) Jedidiah
d) Jeroboam

285. What did God promise to Jeroboam if he would obey him?

a) He would make him ruler over all of Israel.
b) He would protect his kingdom from enemies.
c) He would grant him an enduring dynasty.
d) He would restore his wealth.

286. What was Jeroboam guilty of?
a) Committing adultery
b) Killing innocent people when he was king
c) Worshiping idols
d) None of the above

287. Which prophet cursed King Jeroboam with leprosy for his idolatry?
a) Ahijah
b) Elisha
c) Samuel
d) Isaiah

ELIJAH

This chapter focuses on the biblical prophet Elijah, one of the most prominent figures in the Old Testament. As a messenger from God, Elijah confronted many kings and rulers who ignored his warnings about their wickedness. He also performed numerous miracles to demonstrate God's power over false gods and prophets. We will ask questions about his successor, what he did to show God's power at Mount Carmel, and more!

Bible Trivia

288. What is the name of Elijah's father?
a) Zechariah
b) Elisha
c) Ahab
d) It is not established.

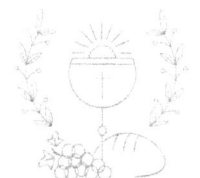

289. What did Elijah do to show God's power over the prophets of Baal?
a) He defeated them in battle.
b) He challenged them to a foot race.
c) He prophesied rain after years of drought.
d) He called down fire from heaven.

290. What is the name of Elijah's successor and student?
a) Jehu
b) Elisha
c) Amos
d) Isaiah

291. Where does Elijah go when he is running from Queen Jezebel?
a) Egypt
b) Beersheba
c) Jerusalem
d) Mount Olympus

292. What happened on Mount Horeb (Sinai), where Elijah went for refuge after running away from Queen Jezebel?
a) The Lord appeared in wind, earthquake, and fire.
b) He encountered an angel who gave him food and drink.
c) He was given instructions to go back and anoint Hazael as king.
d) All of the above.

293. What was the first thing Elijah did when he left Mount Horeb?
a) Anointed Elisha to be his successor
b) Confronted King Ahab
c) Challenged the prophets of Baal
d) Prophesied rain after years of drought

294. How did Elijah divide the waters of the Jordan River?
a) He prayed to God, and a path opened in the river.
b) He used stones to build a dam.
c) He struck it with his staff.
d) None of the above.

295. What was the name of the widow who provided hospitality to Elijah during a time of drought?
a) Samantha
b) Ruth
c) Jessica
d) The widow of Zarephath

296. How did Elijah ascend into heaven?
a) On an angel's chariot
b) By himself in fire and smoke
c) By flying on eagle wings
d) In a whirlwind

297. What did Elisha ask of Elijah before he ascended into heaven?
a) To stay with him
b) Lead the prophets of Baal
c) Inherit a double portion of his spirit
d) For all the wisdom in the world

298. Where did Elijah prove God's power over the prophets of Baal?
a) Mount Sinai
b) Mount Carmel
c) In a river
d) None of the above

299. What was significant about the cloak that fell off Elijah's shoulders when he ascended to heaven?
a) It was indestructible.
b) It was invisible.
c) It gave its wearer miraculous powers.
d) It was picked up by Elisha.

300. Who appeared with Elijah during the transfiguration of Jesus according to the New Testament?

a) An angel
b) Moses
c) Samuel
d) Elisha

Bible Trivia

ELISHA

This chapter covers the life of Elisha, a prophet who succeeded Elijah as God's messenger. We will ask questions about some of his miracles and what happened after he was mocked. Remember, the answers to the questions can be found at the end of the book!

301. What was the first miracle Elisha performed when he succeeded Elijah as a prophet?
   a) The healing of Naaman's leprosy
   b) Purifying a town's water
   c) Parting of the Jordan River
   d) Resurrecting a widow's son

302. Who sent Naaman to Elisha for him to be cured of his disease?
   a) His wife
   b) The King of Aram
   c) Elijah
   d) None of the above

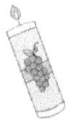    

303. What happened to Gehazi after he disobeyed Elisha and lied to Naaman about taking gifts from him?
   a) He became king.
   b) He died.
   c) He and his descendants were cursed with leprosy.
   d) His house was destroyed.

304. What kind of oil did Elisha ask the Shunammite woman to borrow from her neighbors?
   a) Olive oil
   b) Coconut oil
   c) Flaxseed oil
   d) Hemp seed oil

305. How many men did Elisha feed during the famine?
a) Twelve
b) Seven
c) One hundred
d) None of the above

306. Where was Elijah taken up into heaven in a whirlwind, leaving his mantle behind for Elisha?
a) The Jordan River
b) Mount Horeb
c) The wilderness of Damascus
d) Mount Sinai

307. How many youths mocked Elisha?
a) Five
b) Forty-two
c) Twenty-three
d) None of the above

308. What did Elisha do at Bethel after he was mocked for his baldness?
a) He called down a curse in the name of God.
b) He parted the Jordan River to get away.
c) He fled.
d) He cried.

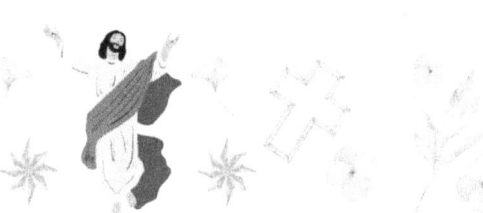

309. Who invited Elisha into his home for a meal after the prophet had performed many miracles in the city?
a) King David
b) Abimelech
c) Naaman
d) The Shunammite Woman

310. What did Elisha throw into the bitter waters to make them sweet at Jericho?
a) Salt
b) Honey
c) Oil
d) Ashes

311. Who was sent by God to anoint Jehu as the king of Israel and Hazael as the king of Syria?
a) Elijah
b) Ezra
c) Jeremiah
d) Elisha

312. How long did Elisha stay with Elijah before he ascended into heaven?
a) Seven days
b) Thirty days
c) Forty days
d) It is not specified.

313. How did Elisha cure Naaman's leprosy?
   a) He told Naaman to bathe in the Jordan River seven times.
   b) He washed his body with special oils.
   c) He had him fast for forty days.
   d) He made Naaman pray for three days and three nights.

314. Whose sons did Elisha ask to borrow two empty vessels, which he then filled with oil?
   a) Ruth
   b) Naomi
   c) Abigail
   d) The Shunammite Woman

KINGS OF JUDAH AND ISRAEL

This chapter covers the kings of Judah and Israel from the period when the kingdoms were divided until the Babylonian captivity. We will explore the rulers and their reigns, as well as some important events.

315. Who succeeded King Jehoram as ruler in the kingdom of Israel?
a) Jehu
b) Omri
c) Ahaziah
d) Nadab

316. Which prophet oversaw the anointing of King Jehu?
a) Elijah
b) Elisha
c) Samuel
d) Ezekiel

317. What is the name of the queen who seized the throne after the death of Ahaziah of Judah and ordered the killing of those who could have contested her rule?
a) Jezebel
b) Athaliah
c) Bathsheba
d) Abigail

318. How many kings reigned in Judah during the period between the division of the kingdom and Babylonian captivity?
a) Twenty
b) Eleven
c) Twelve
d) Fifteen

319. Who succeeded King Ahaz as the ruler of Judah after his death?
a) Josiah
b) Hezekiah
c) Amon
d) Pekah

320. Who was the only surviving son of King Ahaziah who eventually became the eighth king of Judah?
a) Joash
b) Amaziah
c) Jehoram
d) Uzziah

321. Who was responsible for fortifying the walls of Jerusalem?
a) Hezekiah
b) Uzziah
c) Ahaz
d) John

322. Who succeeded King Jeroboam in Israel after his death?
a) Nadab
b) Baasha
c) Zimri
d) Omri

323. What is the name of the northern kingdom established by King Jeroboam following Solomon's death?
a) Judah
b) Benjamin
c) Ephraim
d) Israel

324. Which king, according to 2 Chronicles, stoned his son-in-law, Prophet Zechariah to death, for challenging his authority?
a) Uzziah
b) Hezekiah
c) Joash
d) None of the above

325. Who succeeded King Zimri as ruler of Israel after his assassination?
a) Omri
b) Baasha
c) Pekah
d) Ahaziah

326. Who was the last king of Judah before the Babylonian captivity?
a) Zedekiah
b) Jehoiakim
c) Hezekiah
d) Manasseh

327. What foreign power overthrew and destroyed Jerusalem, ending the Kingdom of Judah?

a) Assyrian Empire
b) Hittite Empire
c) Persian Empire
d) Babylonian Empire

328. Who succeeded King Jeroboam II as ruler of Israel after his death?

a) Zechariah
b) Shallum
c) Pekah
d) Hoshea

329. Which prophet warned against disobeying God's laws during King Jeroboam II's rule?

a) Elijah
b) Elisha
c) Jeremiah
d) Amos

330. Which king of Israel was killed by Jehu in a coup as an act of revenge?

a) Baasha
b) Zimri
c) Nadab
d) Jehoram

331. According to 2 Kings 18:1-4, which king removed all idols from Judah and reinstituted worship only for God?

a) Asa
b) Hezekiah
c) Amon
d) Josiah

332. Who is referred to as "the wicked queen" in the Bible due to her support for idolatry?

a) Athaliah
b) Jezebel
c) Abigail
d) Bathsheba

PROPHETS OF THE OLD TESTAMENT

The Old Testament is full of prophets who communicated God's will to his people. Many individuals were called upon by God to guide his people through difficult times. What did Amos preach against? What did Zechariah prophesy? In this section, we'll explore these questions and more as we examine some of the key prophets from the Old Testament.

333. Who wrote the Book of Lamentations in the Bible?

a) Jeremiah
b) Isaiah
c) Job
d) Ezekiel

334. Which prophet predicted God would restore Israel and Judah into one kingdom?

a) Jeremiah
b) Nahum
c) Habakkuk
d) Zephaniah

335. What were among the main themes of Amos' prophecies?

a) Injustice
b) Repentance
c) Greediness
d) All of the above

336. Which of these prophets saw visions during their service for God?

a) Micah
b) Zechariah
c) Ezekiel
d) All of the above

337. Who prophesied that God would send a shepherd to lead his people?

a) Isaiah
b) Jeremiah
c) Hosea
d) Amos

338. According to the Old Testament, which of the following prophets was swallowed by a giant sea creature for three days and three nights?

a) Obadiah
b) Jonah
c) Micah
d) Nahum

339. What is the main content of the Book of Zechariah?

a) Sinfulness of Israelites
b) The end of the Babylonian captivity
c) The day of judgment
d) The End Times

340. Who is considered to be both a prophet and priest in the Old Testament?

a) Deborah
b) Eli
c) Obadiah
d) Samuel

341. Which country did Jonah come from?
a) Syria
b) Israel
c) Egypt
d) Assyria

342. Which prophet spoke out against those who worshiped other gods?
a) Hosea
b) Jeremiah
c) Ezekiel
d) All of the above

THE BABYLONIAN CAPTIVITY

The Babylonian captivity was a period of Jewish history that began in 586 BCE when the king of Babylon captured Jerusalem and forced the Jews into exile. This section asks questions about how long they remained in captivity, as well as who prophesied an end to it.

343. What was the name of the king of Babylon who captured Jerusalem and took Jews into exile?

a) Nebuchadnezzar II
b) Darius I
c) Cyrus the Great
d) Sargon II

344. How many years did the Jewish people remain in captivity in Babylon?

a) Seventy years
b) Fifty years
c) Twenty-five years
d) Five years

345. Who prophesied that there would be an end to the Babylonian captivity after so many years?

a) Ezekiel
b) Jeremiah
c) Isaiah
d) Habakkuk

346. What event ultimately brought about an end to the Jews' exile?

a) The Exodus
b) The destruction of Solomon's Temple
c) Babylon's war with Persia
d) The return of King Josiah

347. Why were captives taken away into exile by the Babylonian king?

a) To serve as slaves
b) As punishment for not paying tribute
c) To spread the Babylonian culture
d) As a punishment for disobeying God

348. Which book talks about how Daniel interpreted dreams while he was in exile?

a) The Book of Job
b) The Book of Daniel
c) The Book of Isaiah
d) The Book of Jeremiah

349. Who brought about an end to the Jews' exile from Babylon?

a) King Josiah
b) Cyrus the Great
c) Darius I
d) Nebuchadnezzar II

350. Who was the leader of the Jews who were taken into captivity in Babylon?

a) Ezekiel
b) Jehoiachin
c) Zephaniah
d) Mordecai

351. What did some Jews in captivity believe was a sign they would soon be released from exile?

a) The destruction of Babylon
b) A vision given to Daniel
c) The fall of King Nebuchadnezzar II
d) An oracle spoken to by Jeremiah

352. Which book first mentions the beginning of the rebuilding of the Second Temple of Jerusalem after the return from Babylonian captivity?

a) The Book of Zechariah
b) The Book of Chronicles
c) The Book of Samuel
d) The Book of Ezra

353. What was the relationship of Zedekiah, the last King of Judah, to Jehoiachin?

a) He was Jehoiachin's brother
b) He was Jehoiachin's uncle
c) He was Jehoiachin's son
d) He was Jehoiachin's father

354. When were the Jewish people allowed to return to Jerusalem?

a) 538 BCE
b) 620 BCE
c) 612 BCE
d) 655 BCE

355. According to the Bible, who was the first appointed Babylonian governor of Judah?
   a) Jeremiah
   b) Ahikam
   c) Isaiah
   d) Gedaliah

356. Which book of the Bible is mainly about rebuilding the temple and walls in Jerusalem by Zerubbabel?
   a) Exodus
   b) Daniel
   c) Leviticus
   d) Nehemiah

357. Who was the leader who led the Jews back to Jerusalem after the end of Babylonian captivity?
   a) Moses
   b) Zerubbabel
   c) Ezekiel
   d) David

358. How many years did it take for the Jews to rebuild the temple after their return from exile in Babylon?
   a) Three years
   b) Twenty years
   c) Ten years
   d) More than forty years

359. How were the Jews able to rebuild the temple and walls in Jerusalem after the Babylonian captivity?

a) They did not rebuild the temple.
b) King Cyrus helped by providing funds.
c) The Jewish people had hidden their wealth.
d) Their neighbors built the temple and walls.

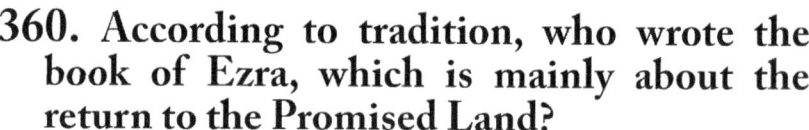

360. According to tradition, who wrote the book of Ezra, which is mainly about the return to the Promised Land?

a) Isaiah
b) Jeremiah
c) Nehemiah
d) Ezra

361. Who was the priest who led the return of the Jews from the Babylonian captivity with Prince Zerubbabel?

a) Jeremiah
b) Joshua
c) Ezra
d) None of the above

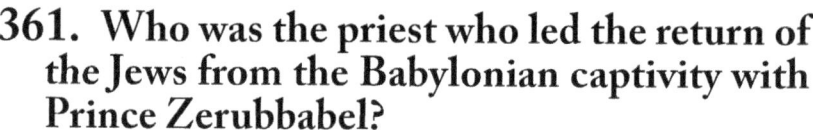

362. How many people went back to Jerusalem under Zerubbabel's leadership?

a) More than forty thousand
b) Fewer than thirty thousand
c) About ten thousand
d) Fewer than twenty thousand

363. What does the term "Jubilee" refer to in the Bible?

a) A period when the people were allowed to return home and some of their debts were forgiven
b) A festival celebrated every seven years for the people's freedom
c) A yearly celebration commemorating the Jewish people's return from exile
d) The day Cyrus captured Babylon

Bible Trivia

ESTHER AND THE PURIM STORY

The following section is about the biblical history of one of the biggest Jewish holidays—Purim. Answer questions about the Achaemenid rule of Judah and other details about Purim; the answers for this section can be found in the Book of Esther.

364. What did Mordecai ask Esther to do when he found out about the king's plans?
a) Stand up for her people and save them from destruction
b) Retreat in fear and do not oppose the king's orders
c) Kill the king
d) Go into hiding so she would be safe

365. In what century did Xerxes (known as Ahasuerus in the Bible) rule Persia?
a) 4th century BCE
b) 5th century BCE
c) 6th century BCE
d) 7th century BCE

366. How many times did the king hold a banquet in Esther's honor?
a) Two times
b) Three times
c) Four times
d) Five times

367. What position was Haman given by King Ahasuerus (Xerxes)?
a) Chief advisor to the king
b) Advisor to the queen
c) Chief eunuch
d) Chief sorcerer

368. Which food or beverage is traditionally consumed in excess on Purim as part of the festive meal?

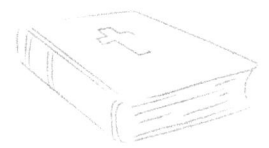

a) Challah bread
b) Wine
c) Falafel
d) Matzoh ball soup

369. Why were people commanded to send gifts to one another on Purim according to the Book of Esther?

a) To remember God's mercy
b) To celebrate the victory of Mordecai and Esther
c) To show kindness to strangers
d) As a sign of repentance

370. Which queen was banished in the Book of Esther for disobeying the orders of King Ahasuerus?

a) Vashti
b) Esther
c) Helena
d) Michal

371. What did Queen Esther ask the Jews to do for three days before she approached the king?

a) Fast and pray
b) Offer sacrifices
c) Celebrate with feasting
d) Worship idols

372. What is peculiar about the Book of Esther?

a) It is the shortest of the books that make up the Old Testament.
b) It is one of only two books in the Bible that don't mention "God."
c) It was the latest book to be discovered.
d) It was the only biblical book written in Hebrew and Aramaic.

373. Which book in the Bible tells us about Esther and her relationship with King Ahasuerus?

a) Exodus
b) Numbers
c) Esther
d) Daniel

374. Which of the following did Mordecai refuse to comply with when it was decreed by Haman?

a) Praying to pagan gods
b) Bowing down before him
c) Wearing the royal robes
d) Paying taxes

375. What is Purim, according to Jewish tradition?

a) A day of fasting and repentance
b) An annual celebration in honor of Queen Esther
c) The anniversary of King Xerxes's ascension
d) A festival commemorating God's deliverance from destruction

Bible Trivia

BIRTH OF JOHN THE BAPTIST

This section asks questions about John the Baptist, a man revered in Christianity. Do you know who John the Baptist's father was? Or how he was related to Jesus? If you ever get stuck, check the answers at the end of the book!

376. What was the name of John's father?
a) Zechariah
b) Joseph
c) Gabriel
d) Saul

377. What was the response of John the Baptist's parents when they found out about his birth?
a) Disbelief
b) Joy
c) Fear
d) Shock

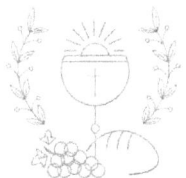

378. Zechariah had doubts when he heard the angel telling him that his and Elizabeth's barrenness would be broken. Why did he doubt the angel?
a) They were advanced in age.
b) He didn't trust the angel.
c) Malachi had prophesied something else.
d) None of the above.

379. What happened after Zechariah questioned Gabriel's message?
a) He was struck dumb.
b) He praised God.
c) He left Jerusalem.
d) He went on a pilgrimage.

380. How long was Zechariah affected because of his disbelief?

a) One month
b) Six months
c) Nine months
d) One year

381. Who told Mary that Elizabeth had miraculously conceived a child in her old age?

a) An angel
b) The priest
c) Elizabeth herself
d) None of the above

382. How many months were there between when Jesus was conceived and when John the Baptist was conceived?

a) One month
b) Two months
c) Six months
d) Eight months

383. In the Bible, John the Baptist and Jesus are related. What was their relationship?

a) Brother
b) Cousin
c) Stepbrother
d) Uncle and nephew

384. After hearing about Elizabeth's pregnancy, what did Mary do?
a) She doubted Elizabeth's honesty.
b) She stayed with her cousin for three months.
c) She left for Nazareth.
d) She told everyone in town.

385. What was the response of those who heard about the birth of John?
a) They praised God.
b) They were afraid.
c) They rejected him.
d) They mocked him.

386. What did John's father do when he first saw his son?
a) He praised God.
b) He laughed with joy.
c) He cried tears of joy.
d) He turned away in disgust.

THE ANNUNCIATION TO THE BLESSED VIRGIN

This section explores one of the most important moments in Christian history. This is the moment when Mary was visited by an angel who announced to her that she would conceive a son through immaculate conception. We will learn about this angel's appearance and his words to Mary, as well as why God chose Mary for this unique task.

387. Which Gospel recounts the story of the Annunciation?
a) The Gospel of John
b) The Gospel of Luke
c) The Gospel of Mark
d) None of the above

388. Who told Joseph about Mary's conception?
a) An angel
b) A wise man
c) Herod
d) Elizabeth

389. According to the Gospel of Matthew, what name for the baby did the angel who appeared suggest to Mary?
a) David
b) Emmanuel
c) Solomon
d) Moses

390. What was the name of Jesus' father?
a) Joseph
b) Martin
c) Jonathan
d) Zechariah

391. What did the angel say to Mary at the Annunciation?

a) "Good luck in the future."
b) "Your son will be a terrible leader."
c) "Do not be afraid, for you have found favor with God."
d) "I am here to bring good news about your future."

392. Where did this event take place?

a) In Nazareth
b) In Bethlehem
c) At Mount Horeb
d) In Jerusalem

393. How did Joseph initially react when he learned about Mary's pregnancy?

a) He became enraged.
b) He wanted to divorce her.
c) He trusted in the Lord.
d) He refused to believe it.

394. What was the name of the angel that appeared to Mary during the Annunciation?

a) Gabriel
b) Michael
c) Raphael
d) Jehoel

395. What did the angel tell Mary about her unborn son?
a) He will be great and will be called the Son of God.
b) His kingdom will fall.
c) He will save people from their sins.
d) He would bring peace to the earth.

396. What is the feast day for celebrating the Annunciation to the Blessed Virgin Mary?
a) Christmas Eve
b) Easter Sunday
c) The Feast of the Annunciation
d) Ascension Thursday

397. After hearing that she would give birth to a son, how did Mary respond?
a) She was afraid.
b) She accepted willingly.
c) She refused.
d) She asked for further clarification.

398. What is the significance of this event in Christianity?
a) It marks the beginning of Jesus' life on earth.
b) It celebrates God's grace and mercy.
c) It symbolizes obedience and faithfulness to God.
d) It demonstrates love between two people.

399. On what date is the Feast of the Annunciation celebrated in most Christian churches today?

a) April 9th
b) April 1st
c) March 25th
d) March 20th

400. According to Luke 1:28, what did the angel say when he greeted Mary?

a) "Hail full of grace!"
b) "Blessed are you among women."
c) "Peace be with you."
d) None of the above.

401. Who was present at the Annunciation according to Luke?

a) Elizabeth, Gabriel, and Joseph
b) Mary and Gabriel
c) Joseph, Zachariah, and Mary
d) Elizabeth, Gabriel, and Mary

JESUS' BIRTH

This chapter explores the birth of Jesus as recorded in the Bible. It begins with the prophecy about where the Messiah would be born and ends when he was first presented to the temple. Answer questions about the Wise Men, and discover who was the king at the time of Jesus' birth. This was one of the most important moments in Christianity; let's see if you know your stuff!

402. Which prophet foretold the birthplace of the Messiah before his birth?

a) Micah
b) Jeremiah
c) Ezekiel
d) Daniel

403. Which Gospels record the story of Jesus' birth?

a) John and Mark
b) Mark and Matthew
c) Matthew and Luke
d) None of the above

404. Where did Mary give birth to baby Jesus according to the Bible?

a) In an inn
b) At her home in Nazareth
c) In a stable in Bethlehem
d) On her way back home from Egypt

405. How did the angels announce the birth of Jesus?

a) They shouted from heaven.
b) They appeared in dreams to Joseph and Mary.
c) An angel told shepherds nearby.
d) All of the above.

406. For what Christian holiday does the Nativity of Jesus serve as the basis?

a) Pentecost
b) Christmas
c) Advent
d) None of the above

407. What star guided the Wise Men from the East to find baby Jesus?

a) The Star of Bethlehem
b) The North Star
c) Sirius
d) Polaris

408. How many wise men came to visit baby Jesus?

a) Two
b) Three
c) Four
d) Five

409. According to the Gospels, whose descendant was Jesus through Joseph?

a) King David
b) Moses
c) Prophet John
d) None of the above

410. What did Mary wrap baby Jesus in, according to Luke 2:7?

a) Clothes spun from the finest silk
b) A strip of animal skin
c) Swaddling bands
d) A blanket

411. What were some gifts brought by the Wise Men for baby Jesus according to the Bible?

a) Frankincense, gold, and myrrh
b) Silver, gold, and spices
c) A sheep, a camel, and a goat
d) Clothes, food, and toys

412. Who was the king when Jesus was born?

a) King David
b) King Saul
c) King Solomon
d) King Herod

413. After baby Jesus' birth, what happened on the eighth day, according to the Bible?

a) The king saw him.
b) He had his circumcision ceremony.
c) He was taken to Syria.
d) None of the above.

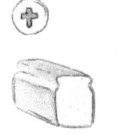

414. Why did Joseph have to take Mary and Jesus away to Egypt shortly after his birth?
a) To escape King Herod, who wanted to kill Jesus
b) To fulfill a prophecy that said he should go there
c) To find a better place to raise Jesus
d) None of the above

415. What animal did Mary ride on when she was traveling to Bethlehem?
a) Camel
b) Donkey
c) Horse
d) Elephant

416. According to the Gospel of Matthew, what does the name Emmanuel mean?
a) God with us
b) Praise the Lord
c) The chosen one
d) None of the above

417. What did Joseph do with Jesus when King Herod died?
a) He took Jesus back to Bethlehem.
b) He stayed in Egypt.
c) He moved to Nazareth.
d) None of the above.

418. How old was Jesus when he was presented at the temple according to Luke 2:22-24?

a) Eight days old
b) Forty days old
c) Three years old
d) Six weeks old

BAPTISM OF JESUS

The baptism of Jesus is an important event in the life and teachings of Christianity. This section explores the significance of this highly symbolic act, as well as its implications for believers today. We will explore questions such as what river Jesus was baptized in and who was present when he was baptized. By answering these questions, we can gain greater insight into a central Christian teaching—the power and importance of being baptized to be saved from sin!

419. In what river did John the Baptist baptize Jesus?

a) Tigris River
b) Jordan River
c) Nile River
d) Euphrates River

420. What words were spoken by God when he revealed himself to Jesus at his baptism?

a) "This is my beloved Son."
b) "My grace is sufficient for you."
c) "You are worthy of me, my son."
d) "Take up your cross and follow me."

421. Who was present when Jesus was baptized?

a) John the Baptist and the Holy Spirit
b) Joseph and Herod Antipas
c) The Twelve Disciples
d) Nicodemus and Simon Peter

422. How old was Jesus at the time of his baptism?

a) Around twelve years old
b) Around thirty years old
c) Around twenty years old
d) Around forty years old

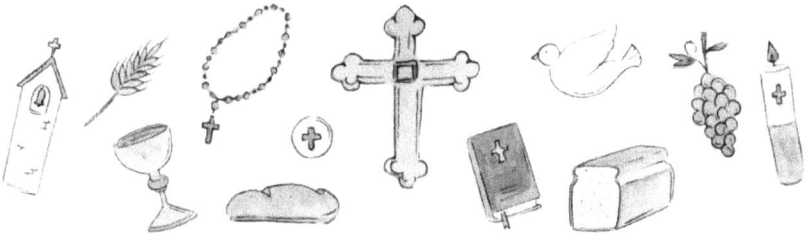

423. Which of the following is not a reason why Jesus was baptized?

a) To show God's favor toward him
b) To fulfill all righteousness
c) To prove his divinity
d) To begin teaching and preaching

424. What happened when Jesus came out of the water after being baptized by John?

a) He heard an audible voice from heaven.
b) He began to preach about repentance.
c) The Spirit of God descended upon him.
d) Angels appeared around him.

425. Which one of these statements best describes what baptism symbolized for Jesus' ministry?

a) It marked the beginning of his earthly mission.
b) It showed his physical superiority.
c) It demonstrated his love for his earthly parents.
d) It signified an important historical moment for Jews.

426. What did John the Baptist say when Jesus asked to be baptized?

a) "I need to be baptized by you, and do you come to me?"
b) "Thou art my beloved Son; in thee I am well pleased."
c) "Repent, for the kingdom of heaven is at hand."
d) None of the above

427. What does it mean that Jesus submitted himself to baptism even though he was sinless?

a) It showed humility and obedience.
b) He wanted others to follow him.
c) He wanted people to know that he had no sin.
d) He needed forgiveness from God.

428. Who witnessed the Holy Spirit descending upon Jesus at his baptism?

a) The Twelve Disciples
b) Nicodemus and Joseph
c) Herod Antipas and Mary Magdalene
d) John the Baptist

429. How might one explain why John initially refused to baptize Jesus?

a) Because he felt unworthy
b) Because it wasn't part of their custom
c) Because he didn't believe Jesus was the Messiah
d) Because it wasn't part of Jesus' mission

430. Why did John baptize people with water?

a) To demonstrate repentance
b) To symbolically cleanse them from sin
c) To identify followers of God
d) To show his loyalty to Caesar

431. Of the canonical Gospels, which contains a different account of the baptism of Jesus?
a) Matthew
b) Mark
c) Luke
d) John

432. What did John the Baptist proclaim when he saw Jesus coming toward him for baptism?
a) "Behold, the Lamb of God!"
b) "This is my beloved Son in whom I am well pleased."
c) "Repent, for the kingdom of heaven is at hand."
d) "You are worthy to receive my baptism."

433. How were those who sought out John's baptism different from those who followed Jesus?
a) They were seeking forgiveness through confession and repentance.
b) They accepted that they could never be good enough by themselves.
c) They believed that their sins had already been washed away.
d) They were looking for a prophet of God.

434. What does it mean when someone is baptized according to Christian tradition?

a) It symbolizes death and rebirth.
b) It signifies repentance and forgiveness.
c) It demonstrates loyalty to Christ.
d) All of the above.

MINISTRY AND MIRACLES OF JESUS

From turning water into wine to healing the sick, this section will explore the miracles and ministry of Jesus Christ. We will examine how his mission on earth was fulfilled through acts of compassion, love, mercy, grace, and power that left those who experienced them in awe. Get ready to dive deep into scripture as we unravel questions about this period of Jesus' life.

Bible Trivia

435. What was Jesus' first miracle?

a) Turning water into wine
b) Feeding five thousand people
c) Healing a blind man
d) Raising Lazarus from the dead

436. According to Luke 4:18-19, what was Jesus' mission on earth?

a) To preach and teach about God's kingdom
b) To be an example of how to live a good life
c) To bring peace among all nations
d) None of the above

437. How did Jesus respond when his disciples asked him for permission to call down fire from heaven in Luke 9:51-56?

a) He granted them their wish.
b) He warned them not to do it.
c) He reprimanded them.
d) He stayed silent.

438. What did Jesus say to the paralytic man in Matthew 9:1-8?

a) "Stand up and walk!"
b) "Your sins are forgiven."
c) "I am here for you."
d) "You have been healed."

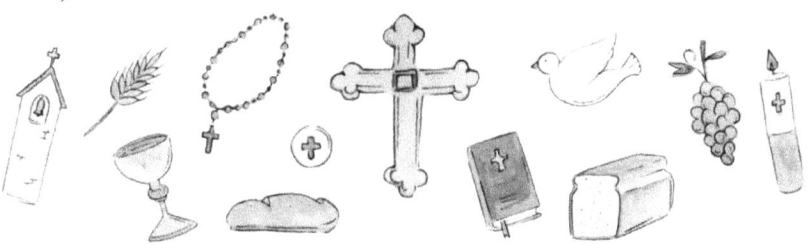

439. Where does the Book of Matthew say most of Jesus' miracles were performed?

a) Jerusalem
b) Nazareth
c) Capernaum
d) Bethany

440. For how many days had Lazarus been dead before he was resurrected by Jesus?

a) Seven
b) Ten
c) Three
d) Four

441. How did Jesus respond when he was asked to pay the temple tax in Matthew 17:24–27?

a) He paid his and Peter's tax with a four-drachma coin.
b) He refused to pay.
c) He asked his disciples to pay it for him.
d) None of the above.

442. Where did Jesus' first miracle take place?

a) Jerusalem
b) Cana
c) Bethlehem
d) Tyre

443. Why is Jesus' first miracle significant?

a) The wedding guests were amazed at his powers.

b) Everyone praised God after it happened.

c) The bridegroom believed in him.

d) It demonstrated his glory and holy ability.

444. In John 6:4-15, how many people were fed after Jesus multiplied the loaves and fishes?

a) About five thousand

b) About four thousand

c) About three thousand

d) About two thousand

445. What did Jesus say of Nathanael in John 1:47?

a) "He does not believe I am the Son of God."

b) "He will follow me."

c) "Here truly is an Israelite in whom there is no deceit."

d) None of the above.

446. How did Jesus respond to the woman caught in adultery as recorded in John 8:4-11?

a) He commended her for her bravery.

b) He told her that he did not condemn her.

c) He asked where the man was.

d) None of the above.

447. What did Nicodemus ask Jesus when he visited him at night according to John 3:1-2?
   a) How to receive eternal life
   b) How to healed from his illness
   c) To understand what the Holy Spirit is
   d) To learn more about Jesus' disciples

448. According to the Book of Mark, how many men carried the paralytic man on a mat into the house where Jesus was teaching?
   a) Two men
   b) Three men
   c) Four men
   d) Five men

449. At Capernaum, why was the paralyzed man lowered from an opening made in the ceiling at Jesus' house?
   a) Because Jesus originally did not want to see him
   b) Because Jesus' house was full of his many followers
   c) Because the paralyzed man insisted so
   d) None of the above

450. In Luke 10:25–37, why does the lawyer ask what he must do to inherit eternal life?

a) He wants to learn more about God's plan.

b) He is testing Jesus.

c) He wants to know how to live a good life.

d) He is trying to understand what heaven is.

451. Which Gospel is the only one to recount Jesus' healing of a paralytic man in Bethesda?

a) Mark

b) Luke

c) Matthew

d) John

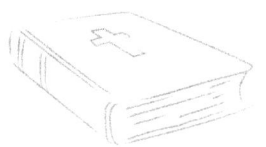

452. What was one way that Jesus provided food for those in need?

a) By turning water into wine

b) By multiplying bread and fish

c) By teaching them how to farm

d) By giving away his own supplies

453. What did Jesus do when merchants were using the temple as a marketplace?

a) He wrote on the ground.

b) He prayed for guidance.

c) He turned over their tables.

d) He did not interact with the,

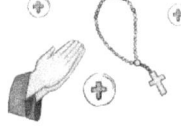

454. How many lepers did Jesus heal during his ministry?
a) One
b) Four
c) Ten
d) Twelve

455. Who was healed of her bleeding after touching the hem of Jesus' garment?
a) Mary Magdalene
b) The Samaritan woman
c) A soldier
d) Jairus's daughter

456. When James and John suggested destroying an entire village that opposed them, what was Jesus' response?
a) He told them to go ahead.
b) He scolded them.
c) He prayed for their souls.
d) He told them to love their enemies.

457. In which Gospel does Jesus tell the Parable of the Good Samaritan?
a) Matthew
b) Mark
c) Luke
d) John

458. Who asked Jesus, "What must I do to inherit eternal life?"

a) The Samaritan woman
b) Nicodemus
c) A rich young man
d) Peter

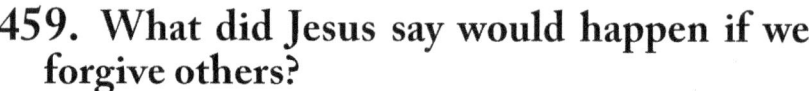

459. What did Jesus say would happen if we forgive others?

a) We will be forgiven in return.
b) Our enemies will love us.
c) Nothing, it's not important.
d) None of the above.

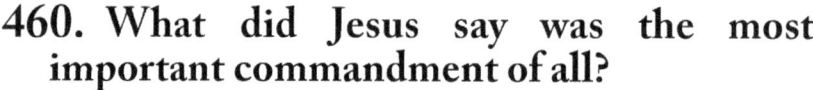

460. What did Jesus say was the most important commandment of all?

a) Love your neighbor as yourself.
b) Honor thy father and mother.
c) Do unto others what you would have them do to you.
d) Love God with all your heart.

461. Who did Jesus give sight to in Mark 8:22-26?

a) A blind man from Bethsaida
b) Two men who had been blind since birth
c) Bartimaeus, a beggar from Jericho
d) Zacchaeus, a tax collector

462. According to John 14:6, what does Jesus state is the only way that leads us back to God?

a) Praying for forgiveness
b) Belief in him
c) Following his teachings
d) The path of truth

463. Where did the story of the loaves and fishes take place?

a) The Garden of Gethsemane
b) On a mountain near Capernaum
c) In the temple courtyard
d) By the Dead Sea

464. Who is known as "the woman at the well" in John 4:1-42?

a) Mary Magdalene
b) Martha
c) Mary of Bethany
d) A Samaritan woman

465. What did Jesus say to Zacchaeus after he repented of his wrongdoings in Luke 19:8-10?

a) Salvation has come to his home today.
b) Believe in me.
c) Follow me to Jerusalem.
d) None of the above.

Bible Trivia

TEMPTATION OF JESUS

In the Bible, Jesus was tempted by Satan in the desert. The story of his temptations is an inspiring example that reflects our own struggles with temptation and provides us with a model to follow if we find ourselves struggling. In this section, we will explore several questions about those temptations, including what Jesus said when he was tempted and how many times Satan attempted to lead him astray.

466. What did Jesus first say when Satan tempted him in the desert?
a) "Let this cup pass from me."
b) "Man shall not live by bread alone, but by every word that proceeds from the mouth of God."
c) "Okay, let's go."
d) "Away from me, Satan!"

467. How many times did Satan try to tempt Jesus according to scripture?
a) Once
b) Twice
c) Three times
d) Eight times

468. Who was with Jesus when Satan attempted to tempt him in the wilderness?
a) His mother
b) Angels
c) His disciples
d) John the Baptist

469. What was one thing Satan promised if Jesus bowed down and worshiped him?
a) Eternal life
b) A happy family
c) Power
d) Nothing

470. In which book is it mentioned that Jesus was tempted in the wilderness?
a) Genesis
b) Lamentations
c) Matthew
d) None of the above

471. For how long did Jesus fast in the Judean desert?
a) A week
b) A month
c) Forty days
d) It is not specified

472. What food did Satan offer as a temptation for Jesus?
a) Fish
b) Locusts
c) Bread
d) Fruits

473. What did Satan challenge Jesus to do during his temptation in the wilderness?
a) Turn stones into bread
b) Worship false idols
c) Take power over all kingdoms of the world
d) None of the above

474. What is one thing that we learn from Christ's example of resisting temptation?
   a) Prayers are useless.
   b) One should always rely on the scripture.
   c) People should put their trust in God.
   d) None of the above.

475. Where did Jesus go after he faced temptation from Satan in the wilderness?
   a) Jerusalem
   b) Mt. Hermon
   c) Galilee
   d) Heaven

476. What was the purpose of Jesus being tempted?
   a) To prove his faith
   b) To test his obedience
   c) To strengthen him
   d) All of the above

Bible Trivia

SERMON ON THE MOUNT

Jesus' Sermon on the Mount is one of the most influential speeches known to man. It was delivered by Jesus to his disciples. This sermon has been studied for centuries as a source of moral guidance and religious instruction, raising questions about its main point, purpose, and impact. Let's explore some questions about the Sermon on the Mount.

477. What is the main point of Jesus' Sermon on the Mount?

a) To teach his disciples about forgiveness
b) To outline the regulations of a new religion
c) To provide instructions for how to live as God intended
d) None of the above

478. In the Bible, on which mountain did Jesus give this sermon?

a) Sinai
b) Hermon
c) Zion
d) It is not specified.

479. Where does Matthew record that Jesus gave this sermon?

a) Near Jerusalem
b) Near Nazareth
c) Near Galilee
d) Near Gethsemane

480. According to biblical scholars, how long was the original version of the Sermon on the Mount?

a) Several days
b) One hour
c) Three months
d) Ten minutes

481. What is the first thing Jesus mentions in his sermon?

a) The Beatitudes
b) Mercy
c) Love
d) Repentance

482. How many Beatitudes does Jesus mention in the Sermon on the Mount?

a) Three
b) Five
c) Eight
d) Nine

483. Which of these is not included among the Beatitude blessings?

a) Those who are persecuted for righteousness's sake
b) Those who mourn
c) Those who hunger and thirst after fame
d) Those who are poor in spirit

484. What did Jesus tell those listening to do if someone wrongs them?

a) Curse them
b) Pray for their enemies
c) Take revenge
d) Forgive them

485. What was the reaction of people when they heard this message from Jesus?
a) They were amazed.
b) They were angry.
c) They were confused.
d) They laughed.

486. How does Jesus describe people who practice what he instructs in the Sermon on the Mount?
a) Fools
b) Hypocrites
c) Righteous
d) Deserving of salvation

487. What is one thing that Jesus encourages believers to do?
a) Be perfect.
b) Love their enemies.
c) Serve others.
d) Follow the law when it works to their benefit.

488. According to Matthew 5:17-18, why did Christ come into this world?
a) To bring salvation
b) To spread love
c) To fulfill the law
d) To judge humanity

489. Who was present during Jesus' Sermon on the Mount?

a) His disciples
b) His mother
c) Angels
d) None of the above

490. How did Jesus describe anger?

a) A sin
b) An emotion to express
c) A necessary response
d) None of the above

491. What is one thing that Jesus says not to do if you want to enter the kingdom of heaven?

a) Love others
b) Repent your sins
c) Seek revenge
d) Obey the law

492. According to Matthew 5:22, what did Jesus mean when he said "Raca?"

a) Idols
b) People with pride
c) An idiot or fool
d) Those who speak against God

493. What did Jesus say about storing treasures on earth?

a) It is wise.
b) It will bring blessings.
c) It should be done in moderation.
d) It should be avoided.

494. What does Jesus suggest that believers do if someone strikes them?

a) Seek revenge.
b) Turn the other cheek.
c) Curse them.
d) Ignore it.

Bible Trivia

PARABLES OF JESUS

Jesus' parables have captivated and inspired people for centuries. Each one contains a lesson that is relevant to our lives today. In this chapter, we will explore these parables and discover their timeless lessons about faith, love, mercy, and justice that still resonate with us today.

495. What is a characteristic feature in each one of Jesus' parables?

a) A moral lesson
b) A humorous anecdote
c) A personified character
d) An allegorical setting

496. What parable did Jesus tell to illustrate the importance of prayer?

a) The Parable of the Good Samaritan
b) The Parable of the Sower
c) The Parable of the Talents
d) The Parable of the Persistent Widow

497. Which parable tells us that God will forgive our sins, no matter how great they are?

a) The Prodigal Son
b) Lazarus and the Rich Man
c) Lost Sheep
d) The Mustard Seed

498. In which parable did Jesus compare himself with a shepherd who seeks after his lost sheep?

a) The Ten Virgins
b) The Great Banquet
c) Lost Sheep
d) Fisherman's Net

499. What was the focus of Jesus' parable about the rich man and Lazarus?

a) The consequences of a life lived without God
b) The power of prayer
c) The reward for faithfulness
d) None of the above

500. In which parable did Jesus illustrate how one should treat one's enemies?

a) Prodigal Son
b) The Mustard Seed
c) Parable of the Talents
d) The Good Samaritan

501. What is an important lesson we can learn from the Parable of the Sower?

a) To invest wisely to reap rewards
b) Not to be deceived by outward appearances
c) To not have hope that people will listen
d) To sow generously with no expectation of return

502. What was the point of Jesus' parable about the rich man and his storehouses?

a) To demonstrate the power of prayer
b) To illustrate how money can buy happiness
c) To emphasize the importance of giving to those in need
d) To warn against hoarding wealth for selfish reasons

503. What is a key lesson we can learn from the Parable of the Good Samaritan?

a) To help those in need regardless of their background or beliefs
b) That material possessions are not important
c) That trust is not important
d) That everyone deserves second chances

504. What was the most important message that Jesus conveyed through the Parable of the Mustard Seed?

a) Do not fear what lies ahead.
b) Miracles can happen with faith.
c) Great things come from small beginnings.
d) Do not be discouraged by obstacles.

505. Which parable taught us the importance of being prepared for what lies ahead?

a) The Parable of the Ten Virgins
b) The Parable of the Talents
c) The Parable of the Prodigal Son
d) The Parable of the Good Samaritan

506. In which parable did Jesus illustrate how one should use their God-given talents?

a) The Parable of the Fisherman's Net
b) The Parable of the Talents
c) The Parable of the Lost Sheep
d) The Parable of the Great Banquet

507. What is an important lesson we can learn from the Parable of the Unmerciful Servant?

a) Forgiveness is essential if we wish to attain salvation.
b) Pride will lead to our downfall.
c) Do not be deceived by outward appearances.
d) Great things come from small beginnings.

508. In which parable did Jesus emphasize the importance of investing wisely?

a) The Parable of the Ten Virgins
b) The Parable of the Talents
c) The Parable of the Prodigal Son
d) The Parable of the Fisherman's Net

509. What is an important message that Jesus conveys through the Parable of the Lost Sheep?

a) We must remain faithful despite temptation.
b) Miracles can happen with faith.
c) Everyone deserves second chances.
d) None of the above.

510. Which parable exemplified how people should treat others as they would like to be treated?

a) Lazarus and the Rich Man
b) Good Samaritan
c) Mustard Seed
d) Parable of the Talents

JESUS' ENTRY INTO JERUSALEM

Join us as we explore the story of Jesus' entry into Jerusalem! How did it all unfold? What does this journey mean for Christians today? Answer questions like these as we uncover the details behind Jesus' entry into Jerusalem.

511. What is the traditional name for Jesus' entry into Jerusalem?

a) The Triumphal Entry
b) Palm Sunday Procession
c) Ascension of Christ
d) Parousia

512. Which animal did Jesus ride on when he entered Jerusalem?

a) Horse
b) Ox
c) Donkey
d) Sheep

513. What was Jesus greeted with in Jerusalem?

a) Stones
b) Palm branches
c) Grapes and figs
d) Gold and silver coins

514. Who spread their cloaks in front of Jesus as he rode into Jerusalem?

a) His disciples
b) Roman soldiers
c) Jewish priests
d) The people of Israel

515. Where did Jesus frequently stay before his visit to Jerusalem?
a) Bethany
b) Rome
c) Antioch
d) None of the above

516. Which Gospels mention this episode from Jesus' life?
a) Mark and Matthew
b) Only John
c) Luke and John
d) All four Gospels

517. Of the following, who accompanied Jesus during his entry into Jerusalem?
a) Lazarus
b) Joseph
c) The disciples
d) None of the above

518. What did some of those present shout when Jesus rode through Jerusalem's gates?
a) "Hosanna!"
b) "Praise be to God!"
c) "Jesus is Lord!"
d) "Go away!"

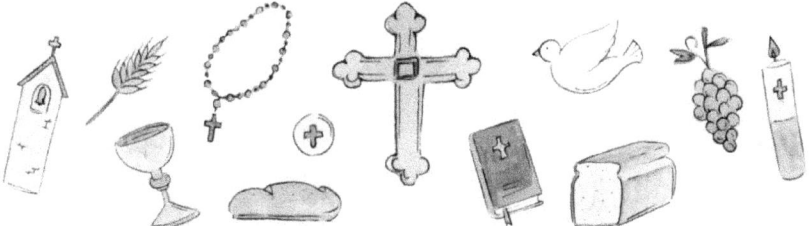

Bible Trivia

519. How many days did Jesus spend in Jerusalem before his arrest and crucifixion?
 a) Two
 b) Three
 c) Four
 d) Five

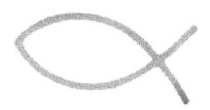

520. Who of these was not with Jesus when he entered Jerusalem?
 a) Mary Magdalene
 b) Thomas
 c) Simon Peter
 d) None of the above

521. According to Luke 19:41, what was Jesus' reaction when he saw Jerusalem?
 a) He wept.
 b) He shouted with joy.
 c) He prayed silently.
 d) He praised God.

522. Where was Jesus coming from when he entered Jerusalem?
 a) Bethlehem
 b) Bethany
 c) Jericho
 d) Capernaum

523. What emotion does the term Hosanna express?
a) Praise
b) Joy
c) Adoration
d) All of the above

524. Which feast was to be celebrated at the time of Jesus' triumphal entry into Jerusalem?
a) Passover
b) Sukkot
c) Purim
d) The Day of Atonement

525. What was the purpose of Jesus' entry into Jerusalem?
a) To begin his ministry
b) To meet with the high priests
c) To preach in local synagogues
d) To celebrate Passover

Bible Trivia

THE LAST SUPPER

The Last Supper is one of the most well-known events in the Bible. It marks Jesus' final meal and his last moments before he was arrested and ultimately crucified. How much do you know about this moment?

526. What do biblical scholars believe Jesus and his disciples ate during the Last Supper?

a) Fish and bread
b) Lamb, unleavened bread, and bitter herbs
c) Pasta
d) Roast beef with potatoes

527. Where was the Last Supper held?

a) In a room on Mount Zion
b) On a mountain near Nazareth
c) In Galilee, by a lake
d) At Herod's palace

528. Who attended the Last Supper?

a) Jesus and all twelve of his disciples
b) Angels
c) Mary Magdalene
d) The Pharisees

529. What did Judas Iscariot do during the Last Supper?

a) He left early.
b) He cried.
c) He gave a sermon.
d) He sang.

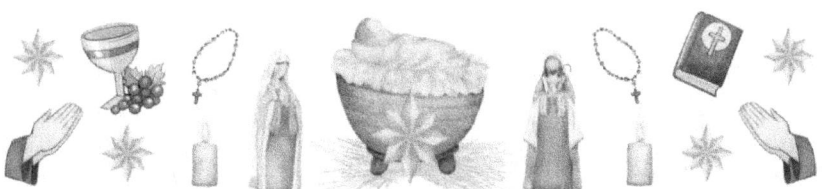

530. What did Jesus do with the bread at the Last Supper?

a) Spat on it
b) Threw it on the floor
c) Blessed it
d) Ate all of it

531. Who dipped their hand in the same dish as Jesus during the Last Supper?

a) Simon Peter
b) Judas Iscariot
c) Andrew
d) John

532. How many cups were used to pass around wine during the Last Supper?

a) One
b) Two
c) Three
d) Four

533. When was the Last Supper held according to biblical accounts?

a) The night before Passover
b) Midnight of Good Friday
c) Dawn Easter Day
d) On Thursday

534. In the Book of John, what did Jesus tell the disciples to do after they ate together at the Last Supper?
   a) Sing praises
   b) Pray for forgiveness
   c) Spread the word of God
   d) To always love one another

535. Where did John lay his head on while eating dinner at the Last Supper?
   a) On Jesus' bosom
   b) On Andrew's shoulder
   c) On the tablecloth
   d) On Matthew's arm

536. How is Judas identified by Jesus in scripture just before he leaves from being at the Last Supper?
   a) As his beloved friend
   b) As the betrayer
   c) As a servant
   d) As a messenger

537. Which important Christian rite was first instituted during the Last Supper?
   a) Liturgy
   b) Eucharist
   c) Confirmation
   d) None of the above

538. What did Jesus use as an example of his body during the Last Supper?
a) A chalice of wine
b) A loaf of bread
c) An olive branch
d) A fish

539. Who was not present at the Last Supper?
a) Mary Magdalene
b) Peter
c) John
d) Judas Iscariot

540. Why was Passover celebrated during the Last Supper?
a) To remember God's protection of his people
b) As an offering to God
c) To honor Jesus
d) For Jesus's birth

541. What did Jesus tell his disciples before he was arrested?
a) To remain faithful
b) To love one another
c) To fight for him
d) Not to worry about him

THE CRUCIFIXION OF JESUS

In this chapter, you will answer questions about Jesus' trial, his sentence, and his suffering on the cross. Who was responsible for ordering Jesus' execution? How many times did Peter deny knowing him after his arrest? Remember, there is an answer key in the back of the book if you get stuck.

542. Who was the Roman ruler who ordered Jesus' crucifixion?

a) Herod Antipas
b) Pontius Pilate
c) Julius Caesar
d) Nero Claudius Caeser

543. How many times did Peter deny knowing Jesus after his arrest?

a) One time
b) Two times
c) Three times
d) Four times

544. According to tradition, on what day of the week was Jesus crucified?

a) Friday
b) Monday
c) Tuesday
d) Wednesday

545. According to Christian tradition, what kind of wood was used to make the cross for Jesus' crucifixion?

a) Cedar
b) Cypress
c) Pine
d) All of the above

546. In the Gospel of Mark, how many times does Jesus predict his own death

a) Two times
b) Three times
c) Four times
d) Five times

547. What color robe did the soldiers put on Jesus during his crucifixion?

a) Red
b) White
c) Blue
d) Purple

548. Who asked Pilate if they could take away Jesus' body after he had died?

a) Mary Magdalene
b) Joseph of Arimathea
c) Simon Peter
d) Nicodemus

549. What were the other criminals that were crucified alongside Jesus charged with?

a) With being thieves
b) With inciting riots
c) With adultery
d) None of the above

550. How long was Jesus on the cross before he died?
a) Three hours
b) Six hours
c) Nine hours
d) Twelve hours

551. According to Luke, what were the last words Jesus spoke on the cross before he died?
a) "Father, forgive them."
b) "It is finished."
c) "I am the son of God."
d) "Father, into thy hands I commend my spirit."

552. Which of the following witnessed Jesus' death?
a) John the Baptist
b) Nicodemus
c) Jesus' mother, Mary
d) Simon Peter

553. What did they offer Jesus to drink while he hung on the cross?
a) Apple Cider
b) Sour Wine
c) Gall
d) Vinegar

554. What title did Pilate give to Jesus when he was crucified?

a) King of the Jews
b) Son of Man
c) Prince of Peace
d) Savior of Israel

555. Which synoptic gospel mentions that the sky suddenly became dark after Jesus' resurrection?

a) Matthew
b) Mark
c) Luke
d) All of them

556. What did Roman soldiers put on Jesus' head before he died?

a) A crown of thorns
b) A white cloth
c) A silly hat
d) None of the above

557. Who said, "Surely, this was the Son of God," when they saw Jesus' crucifixion?

a) The centurion
b) Simon Peter
c) Mary Magdalene
d) Joseph of Arimathea

Bible Trivia

558. Which of the following women followed and witnessed the crucifixion?
a) Martha
b) Mary Magdalene
c) Elizabeth
d) Hannah

559. What did the soldiers do to Jesus' clothes when he was on the cross?
a) Dipped them in vinegar
b) Divided them among themselves
c) Offered them as a gift
d) Burned them

RESURRECTION OF JESUS

The resurrection of Jesus is a foundational belief in Christianity. This section will look at the events leading up to and occurring immediately after his resurrection, such as who moved the stone from his tomb and what language the angels spoke when they appeared there.

560. How long after the crucifixion of Jesus did he rise again?

a) Three days
b) Two weeks
c) One day
d) Five days

561. What is believed to be the first thing that Jesus spoke when he rose from the dead?

a) "Peace be with you."
b) "I am alive!"
c) "It is finished."
d) "Rejoice!"

562. Where was Mary Magdalene when she first encountered the risen Christ?

a) In Jerusalem
b) At home in Galilee
c) At Jesus' tomb
d) None of the above

563. When did Jesus appear to Thomas, according to scripture?

a) After two days
b) Forty days later
c) He did not see Thomas
d) After he had met the other disciples first

564. According to the Bible, how many angels appeared at Jesus' tomb when he rose?
a) One
b) Two
c) Three
d) Four

565. What did Mary of Magdalene tell the disciples after seeing the risen Christ?
a) "Go to Jerusalem."
b) "I have seen him."
c) "Peace be with you."
d) "Go and proclaim it to all nations."

566. Who was sent by God to roll away the stone from Jesus' tomb?
a) An angel
b) Joseph of Arimathea
c) Nicodemus
d) Mary Magdalene

567. Where did Jesus first appear to his disciples after his resurrection?
a) In The Garden of Gethsemane
b) On The Mount of Olives
c) In Nazareth
d) None of the above

568. Who saw two angels in white when Jesus rose from the dead?

a) Mary Magdalene
b) Peter and John
c) Joseph of Arimathea
d) Martha

569. How did the Roman guards react to seeing an angel at Jesus' tomb?

a) They were stupefied.
b) They bowed down.
c) They laughed.
d) They praised God.

570. What was on the stone that had been moved from Jesus' tomb?

a) A sign reading "He is risen!"
b) An inscription of his name
c) Nothing
d) A seal with Pilate's signature

571. According to scripture, who buried Jesus?

a) Joseph of Arimathea
b) Mary Magdalene
c) Nicodemus
d) The Roman Guards

572. What did the angel tell Mary when she came to the tomb looking for Jesus' body?
a) "He has fled."
b) "Do not be afraid."
c) "Go and proclaim it to all nations."
d) "I am an angel sent by God."

573. What year do biblical scholars think Jesus rose from the dead?
a) 30 CE
b) 33 CE
c) 45 CE
d) 70 CE

574. What emotion did Thomas first experience when he was told of Jesus' resurrection?
a) Fear
b) Joy
c) Doubt
d) Anger

Bible Trivia

ASCENSION OF JESUS

The Ascension of Jesus marks the moment when Jesus ascended into heaven. So, how many days did it take place after his resurrection? Where exactly did his disciples see him ascend? These questions and more await you in this section.

575. What did Jesus do after giving his final instructions to the apostles?
a) Prayed for forty days
b) Wept bitterly
c) Proclaimed the Kingdom of God
d) Ascended to heaven

576. How many days after his resurrection did Jesus ascend to heaven?
a) Four days
b) Forty days
c) Three days
d) Seven days

577. Where were the disciples when they saw Jesus ascend into heaven?
a) In Galilee
b) The Bethesda Pool
c) The Mount of Olives
d) The Garden of Gethsemane

578. Of the following, which book directly mentions the events of the Ascension of Jesus?
a) Epistle to the Hebrews
b) Acts
c) Psalms
d) Revelation

579. Which of the Gospels also wrote in detail about his ascension?

a) Matthew
b) Mark
c) Philip
d) Luke

580. How many disciples were present when Jesus ascended to heaven?

a) Four
b) Eight
c) Eleven
d) Twelve

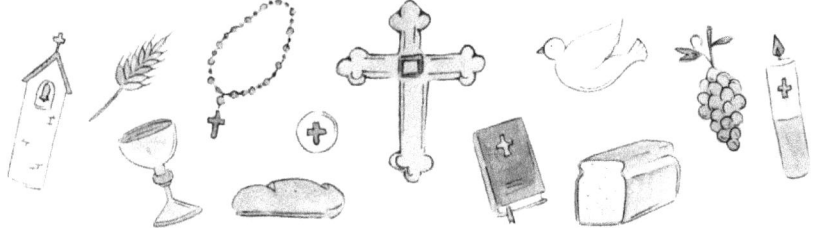

581. Which disciple was not present at Jesus' ascension?

a) Thomas
b) Peter
c) Judas
d) Andrew

582. After ascending, where did two angels instruct the apostles not to leave until they received a gift from above?

a) Rome
b) Jerusalem
c) Nazareth
d) Antioch

583. After Jesus' ascension, what happened to the disciples?

a) They scattered in fear.
b) They were filled with joy.
c) They mourned for days.
d) They continued preaching.

584. When will Christ return according to Christian belief?

a) On Easter Sunday
b) At Pentecost
c) It is not known.
d) As soon as possible

585. According to the Bible, where would Christ reside after his ascension to heaven?

a) Garden of Eden
b) At the right hand of God
c) At the gates of heaven
d) None of the above

586. In which book is there an account of angels speaking about Christ's ascension?

a) Matthew
b) John
c) Mark
d) Acts

587. What was said by the angels when they appeared at the Ascension of Jesus?

a) "Rejoice for he has risen!"
b) "This is our Lord's doing, and it is marvelous in our eyes!"
c) "Behold, he will come again soon!"
d) "This same Jesus shall so come in like manner as ye have seen him go into heaven."

588. Who were the two figures in white clothing seen at Christ's ascension?

a) Angels
b) Disciples
c) Soldiers
d) Pharisees

589. How is Ascension Day celebrated in Christianity?

a) With prayer and fasting
b) By attending church services
c) Through song and dance
d) All of the above

590. What is the significance of Jesus' ascension, according to Christianity?

a) To demonstrate his power
b) To show that he was divine
c) To prove his resurrection
d) All of the above

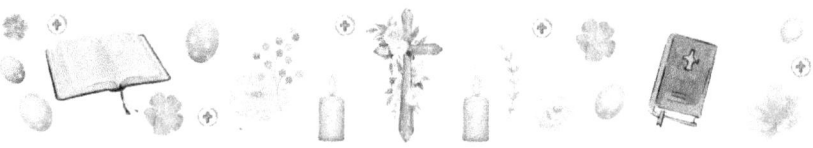

THE DAY OF PENTECOST

An important date on the Christian calendar is Pentecost. It marks a pivotal moment that changed everything for the future of this faith. But what does Pentecost mean? What occurred during this event, and who was involved? Answer these trivia questions about Pentecost!

591. What does the word "Pentecost" mean in Greek?

a) Ten days of preparation
b) Fiftieth
c) The Feast of Weeks
d) Day of Atonement

592. What occurred on Pentecost?

a) The death and resurrection of Jesus Christ
b) The death of John the Baptist
c) Jesus' ascension into heaven
d) The descent of the Holy Spirit

593. How long did it take for the apostles to receive their gift from above after Jesus ascended into heaven?

a) One day
b) Seven days
c) Forty days
d) Ten days

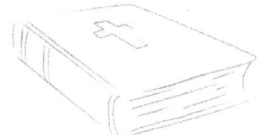

594. What was heard by those who were present during the day of Pentecost?

a) Water droplets
b) An earthquake
c) Noises from heaven
d) Dogs barking

595. Who said, "This is what was spoken by the prophet Joel?"
a) Peter
b) John
c) Paul
d) James

596. According to Acts 2:41, what was the result of Peter's sermon at Pentecost?
a) Around three thousand people were saved from their sins.
b) About five thousand people became followers of Christ.
c) Ten thousand Jews converted to Christianity.
d) Twelve disciples chose to follow Jesus.

597. On which feast does Pentecost occur in Judaism?
a) Shavuot
b) Yom Kippur
c) Passover
d) Rosh Hashanah

598. What happened to those who heard and believed on the day of Pentecost?
a) They were all killed.
b) They were healed of their infirmities.
c) They received the gift of tongues.
d) They received the Holy Spirit.

599. Which bird is believed to be a representation of the Holy Spirit?
   a) Dove
   b) Pigeon
   c) Eagle
   d) Crow

600. What did Peter encourage those who heard him to do?
   a) Repent and be baptized.
   b) Pray only to Jesus.
   c) Obey secular and divine laws.
   d) Turn from God.

601. According to what the prophet Joel said, which physical signs would accompany when the Lord poured out his spirit?
   a) Fire and wind
   b) Rain and hail
   c) Thunder and lightning
   d) Smoke and miracles

602. According to tradition, which of the apostles wrote about this event after it had occurred?
   a) Matthew
   b) Mark
   c) Luke
   d) John

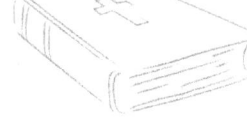

603. What did the apostles do after they received the Holy Spirit?

a) They hid in fear.
b) They prayed and fasted.
c) They preached in the name of God.
d) They fled to Jerusalem.

604. What is not one of the gifts of the Holy Spirit?

a) Understanding
b) Wisdom
c) Piety
d) Luck

605. What did many people of Jerusalem conclude when they heard about the day of Pentecost?

a) It was a miracle.
b) It was an evil spirit.
c) It was the work of Satan.
d) It was just noise.

606. How were those who received the Holy Spirit enabled to do great things?

a) Through their own power
b) Through human intercession
c) Through the gifts of God
d) Through miracles

Bible Trivia

PETER'S MINISTRY AND MIRACLES

In this section, we will explore the life and ministry of one of Jesus' most beloved disciples, Peter. We will look at how he first encountered Jesus, his role as an apostle, and some of the miracles attributed to him during his time with Jesus. Answer more questions more about this important figure who opened a door for Christianity to spread to other nations!

607. How did Peter first encounter Jesus?
a) At a nearby synagogue while praying
b) While casting nets into the Sea of Galilee
c) Through his brother Andrew, who was already one of Jesus' disciples
d) In Jerusalem during Pentecost

608. What event marked the beginning of Peter's ministry as an apostle?
a) The calling of Levi Matthew as an Apostle
b) His participation in feeding 5000 people
c) The day of the Pentecost
d) Seeing Jesus transfigured on Mount Tabor

609. What was the name of Peter's father?
a) Jacob
b) John
c) Simon
d) None of the above

610. After he became one of the twelve apostles, what did Jesus give Peter according to Matthew 16:19?
a) The power to heal the sick
b) The keys to the kingdom of heaven
c) Authority over all his followers
d) Control over a fishing boat

611. What was the first miracle attributed to Peter in Acts 3:1-10?

a) Healing a man who had been lame from birth
b) Raising someone from the dead
c) Turning water into wine
d) Calming a stormy sea

612. What happens in the section of the Bible often referred to as the Restoration of Peter?

a) Jesus forgives Peter for denying him.
b) Peter weeps bitterly and begs for mercy from the soldiers.
c) The disciples welcome Peter back among their ranks.
d) None of the above.

613. Which two prophets appeared to Jesus when he was praying on the mountain with Peter, John, and James, according to Luke 9?

a) Samuel and Ezekiel
b) Elijah and Moses
c) Elijah and Elisha
d) Zechariah and Moses

614. In Acts 3:12-15, what does Peter accuse of the Jews in the Temple?

a) Of being responsible for the death of Jesus
b) Of putting up with the Gentiles
c) Of losing their traditional ways of life
d) All of the above

615. What did Jesus tell Peter before he was arrested and crucified?
a) That his faith would never fail him
b) To go out into the world and preach
c) He will be given great power to heal others
d) That he would deny Jesus three times

616. Who was Cornelius?
a) Roman centurion
b) Roman tax collector
c) Roman teacher
d) None of the above

617. What did Cornelius do when Peter entered his home?
a) He bowed down before Pete.
b) He offered money to buy salvation.
c) He accepted Christ as his savior.
d) He requested that he be baptized immediately.

618. What did Peter tell the Jewish believers when they criticized his decision to preach to Gentiles?
a) That Jesus commanded him to do it
b) That he was obeying God's will
c) That it is wrong for them to judge others
d) That all people should be accepted as equals

619. How did Peter heal a crippled beggar in Acts 3:6-8?

a) By laying hands on him and praying
b) By anointing him with oil
c) By giving him money for food and medicine
d) By casting out demons from within him

620. What did Peter tell the Sanhedrin when they questioned him about his healing of a crippled man?

a) That it was accomplished through Jesus' name
b) That Jesus had commanded him to heal
c) That anyone can be healed if they have faith
d) That only those with great wealth can be healed

621. What did Peter accuse Ananias of doing in Acts 5?

a) Of betraying Jesus with Judas
b) Of killing his own children
c) Of being greedy and stealing money
d) All of the above

622. What did Jesus tell Peter before ascending into heaven?

a) That the Holy Spirit would not come to him
b) To go out into the world and preach
c) To love one another as brothers and sisters in Christ
d) To forgive those who have wronged him

623. How did Peter respond after hearing that Cornelius had received a vision from an angel?

a) He speaks about God's message.
b) He said that it was impossible.
c) He refused to believe it at first.
d) He asked Cornelius why he had been chosen.

624. What event marked the end of Peter's ministry as an apostle?

a) His incarceration and martyrdom
b) The calling of John Mark as an apostle
c) His participation in healing a paralytic man
d) Seeing Jesus ascend into heaven

625. How did Peter die?

a) He was crucified upside down.
b) He was stoned by his enemies.
c) He died from old age after many years of preaching.
d) He drowned while crossing the Sea of Galilee.

Bible Trivia

PAUL'S TRAVELS

Paul is remembered as a great missionary and an influential figure whose travels shaped Christianity in many parts of the world. During his lifetime, Paul took four missionary journeys to spread the gospel. This section asks questions about Paul's travels, including what he encountered along the way and who traveled with him.

626. What was the purpose of Paul's first missionary journey?

a) Planting churches and spreading the gospel to Jews and Gentiles
b) Bringing back Peter from Jerusalem
c) Collecting money for a temple in Jerusalem
d) None of the above

627. How many Pauline epistles are there in total?

a) Seven
b) Ten
c) Twelve
d) Thirteen

628. Who were Barnabas, Silas, Timothy, John Mark, and Luke?

a) Disciples who accompanied Paul on his journeys
b) Roman soldiers sent by Nero to persecute Christians
c) Leaders of Jewish synagogues who opposed Paul's teachings
d) High priests responsible for approving decisions made by the Sanhedrin

629. Which major out of these was founded by Peter?

a) Constantinople
b) Antioch
c) Athens
d) Alexandria

630. Where did Paul famously preach during his second missionary journey?
a) Damascus, Syria
b) Athens, Greece
c) Corinth, Greece
d) Ephesus, Turkey

631. Where was Paul imprisoned during his second missionary journey?
a) Ephesus
b) Rome
c) Corinth
d) Philippi

632. Which of the Pauline epistles is the longest?
a) Galatians
b) Philippians
c) Corinthians
d) Romans

633. What significant event happened during Paul's third missionary journey?
a) He was captured and imprisoned in Rome.
b) He declared Christianity as the official religion of the Roman Empire.
c) The Jerusalem Council met to discuss religious doctrine.
d) It was prophesied that he would be arrested by Gentiles.

634. Who of these accompanied Paul on his fourth and final missionary journey?
a) Luke
b) Peter
c) James
d) Priscilla and Aquila

635. Who of these baptized Paul according to Acts 9?
a) Ananias of Damascus
b) Simon Peter
c) James
d) Philip the Evangelist

636. Where did this last trip take them?
a) Ephesus, Turkey
b) Athens, Greece
c) Corinth, Greece
d) Rome, Italy

637. What city was Luke from?
a) Jerusalem
b) Athens
c) Antioch
d) Damascus

638. Which of these places did Paul not visit during his journeys?

a) Damascus
b) Rome
c) Paris
d) Antioch

639. Who was Philemon, to whom one of the Pauline epistles is addressed?

a) A Roman governor
b) A leader of the Colossian Church
c) A friend of Paul
d) None of the above

640. How did Paul return home from his second journey?

a) By boat
b) On foot
c) By donkey
d) By horseback

641. What was the people's response to Paul's preaching?

a) They were very hostile.
b) Many listened to his message but decided against baptism.
c) No one wanted to listen.
d) He had great success in converting Jews and Gentiles alike.

642. What language is the Pauline Epistle to the Galatians written in?

a) Aramaic
b) Hebrew
c) Latin
d) Koine Greek

643. What is one of the main themes of Paul's letters?

a) Salvation through faith in Jesus Christ
b) The importance of following Jewish law
c) The need to follow religious rituals
d) A call for Christians to live holy lives

644. Paul was headed toward what city when he experienced his famous vision that changed his life?

a) Antioch
b) Damascus
c) Jerusalem
d) Philippi

645. When Saul's name changed, what did he start being called?

a) Paul
b) Peter
c) James
d) John

646. How many letters are attributed to Paul?
a) Thirteen
b) Twelve
c) Ten
d) Twenty

647. Approximately when did Paul and Barnabas go on their first missionary journey?
a) 80 CE
b) 73 CE
c) 46 CE
d) 53 CE

648. Where were Paul and Barnabas sent by the Holy Spirit during that mission trip?
a) Syria
b) Asia Minor
c) Greece
d) None of the above

649. What did Paul and Barnabas do when they encountered resistance from the Jewish community in Iconium?
a) They fled the city
b) Pronounced curses on them
c) Prayed for divine intervention
d) Called upon Roman authorities

650. Where was Paul imprisoned?
a) Damascus
b) Caesarea
c) Jerusalem
d) Antioch

651. What creature attacked Paul on Malta as described in Acts 28:3-6?
a) Scorpion
b) Snake
c) Wolf
d) Eagle

652. According to Acts, what was Paul's occupation before he converted and became an apostle?
a) He was a teacher
b) He persecuted Christians
c) He was a traveler
d) None of the above

653. Which Roman emperor is believed to have been responsible for Paul's execution?
a) Augustus
b) Tiberius
c) Nero
d) Caligula

Bible Trivia

654. Where was Paul buried?
 a) Jerusalem
 b) Antioch
 c) Corinth
 d) Rome

DISCIPLES

Jesus called twelve disciples to follow him and teach the gospel. These men stayed devoted to Jesus despite the many obstacles they faced along the way. In this section, you will explore who was chosen as Christ's disciple and answer questions about their journeys and adventures.

655. Who was the first of Jesus' disciples to be martyred?

a) Peter

b) James the Greater

c) John

d) Andrew

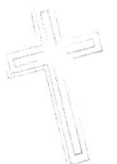

656. How many women followers were among Christ's apostles when he ascended into heaven?

a) Two

b) Three

c) Four

d) None

657. What was the name of the new apostle that replaced Judas Iscariot, according to the Acts?

a) Luke

b) Matthias

c) Saul

d) None of the above

658. What is notable about the calling of Matthew as a disciple by Jesus?

a) That Matthew was a tax collector.

b) It happened during a meal in his home.

c) It was done privately.

d) He was the first one to be called.

659. What did Jesus ask Peter after Peter denied him?
a) "Do you love me more than these?"
b) "Are you ready to follow me?"
c) "Will you stay with me until the end?"
d) "Can I trust you again?"

660. Which apostle wrote the epistles that are included in the New Testament?
a) Paul
b) Peter
c) James
d) All of the above

661. How many pairs of brothers made up Christ's inner circle of disciples?
a) Two
b) Three
c) Four
d) Five

662. What was the name of John's brother who was also a disciple?
a) James
b) Jude
c) Simon
d) Andrew

663. Who is referred to as the "disciple whom Jesus loved?"
a) Peter
b) Judas Iscariot
c) Thomas
d) John

664. Which apostle introduced Nathaniel to Jesus?
a) John
b) Philip
c) Thomas
d) Jude

665. Who was the only apostle who did not believe that Jesus had been resurrected?
a) Peter
b) Thomas
c) John
d) James

666. What was Philip's profession before he became one of Christ's disciples?
a) Fisherman
b) Tax collector
c) Carpenter
d) Physician

667. Who did Jesus call to be the leader of his disciples?

a) Peter
b) John
c) James
d) Judas Iscariot

668. Who was the only apostle who did not die a martyr's death?

a) Peter
b) John
c) James
d) Andrew

669. Who among these heard God's voice at the Jordan River?

a) John the Baptist
b) Peter
c) Judas Iscariot
d) Matthew

670. Who is known as the author of the Hebrews?

a) Unknown
b) James
c) Peter
d) John

671. How was Matthias chosen as a new apostle in place of Judas Iscariot?
a) It was Peter's decision
b) The disciples cast lots
c) According to Jesus' will
d) None of the above

672. Who, out of these, was not one of the original twelve apostles of Jesus?
a) Paul
b) Peter
c) Judas
d) Philip

673. What does the term "Gentiles" refer to?
a) Non-Jewish believers
b) Jewish believers who were not circumcised
c) Jews living outside of Israel
d) None of the above

674. Who is thought to be the first Gentile to convert to Christianity?
a) Cornelius
b) Paul
c) Peter
d) Matthew

675. Who was the first Christian martyr?
a) Stephen
b) James
c) Peter
d) John

676. How did Thomas believe that Jesus had indeed resurrected?
a) Peter made him believe
b) The Holy Spirit communicated it to him
c) He believed once he saw Jesus' wounds from the crucifixion
d) He believed after he prayed for 40 days

677. After Pentecost, what happened when believers devoted themselves to the apostles' teaching?
a) They spoke in tongues.
b) They healed the sick.
c) They preached only to children.
d) The Christian Church was established.

678. What was the first church council held to address issues facing early believers?
a) Jerusalem Council
b) Galatian Council
c) Antioch Council
d) Philippian Conference

679. What was the outcome of this council?
a) Lawful circumcision was required.
b) Gentiles did not have to follow most of the Jewish rules.
c) Jews and Gentiles should separate.
d) Christians should observe Jewish customs.

680. How is Thomas the apostle commonly referred to as?
a) Bald Thomas
b) Doubting Thomas
c) Devout Thomas
d) Great Thomas

681. What was Stephen, the first martyr, accused of by the Sanhedrin?
a) Idolatry
b) Thievery
c) Blasphemy
d) Adultery

682. According to the Epistle to the Colossians, what was the profession of Luke the Evangelist?
a) Physician
b) Teacher
c) Priest
d) None of the above

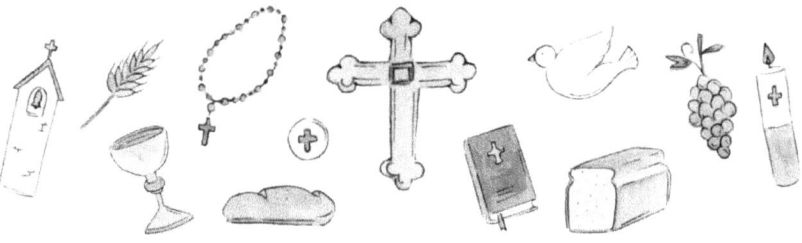

683. What did this council decide regarding Gentile conversion?

a) Gentiles must be circumcised.
b) Gentiles did not need to be circumcised.
c) Jews and Gentiles should remain separate.
d) Converts should always observe Jewish customs.

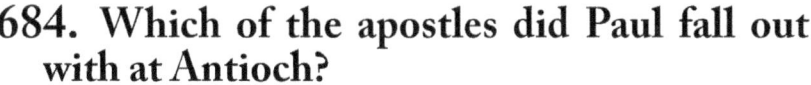

684. Which of the apostles did Paul fall out with at Antioch?

a) James
b) Luke
c) Peter
d) John

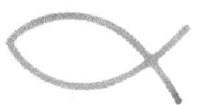

685. What is the name given to the event during which Jesus instructed his disciples to spread the Christian message around the world?

a) The Great Commission
b) The Great Commandment
c) The Great Journey
d) None of the above

Bible Trivia

PERSECUTION OF THE EARLY CHRISTIANS

We have asked a few questions about the persecution of early Christians, but this topic is so important that it deserves its own section. Throughout the long and turbulent history of Christianity, there has been a pattern of persecution. From the Roman Empire to more modern times, those who chose to practice their faith have done so despite potential consequences. In this section, you will be answering questions about Christians who were persecuted for their beliefs.

686. What term is used to describe those who willingly died for their beliefs during times of persecution?

a) Martyrs
b) Heretics
c) Saints
d) Convicts

687. What was the name of the Roman Emperor who first persecuted Christians?

a) Nero
b) Augustus
c) Tiberius
d) Caligula

688. Which book in the Bible tells stories about early Christian persecution and martyrdom?

a) Acts
b) Genesis
c) Revelation
d) Romans

689. Who was responsible for the death of Stephen, the first martyr of Christianity?

a) Gentiles
b) Roman soldiers
c) Jewish Pharisees
d) None of the above

690. Who, among these, participated in the stoning of Stephen?

a) Peter
b) Thomas
c) Judas Iscariot
d) Saul (Paul)

691. How did Polycarp, an early Christian martyr, die?

a) Crucifixion
b) Burned at the stake and stabbed
c) Beheading
d) Stoning

692. How did the Romans treat the Christians before they were sent to their death?

a) They beat them.
b) They treated them decently.
c) They typically poked their eyes out.
d) They often drowned them.

693. What was the Roman Empire's religion before the emergence of Christianity?

a) Buddhism
b) Judaism
c) Paganism
d) Islam

694. What did Emperor Nero blame the Christians?

a) Assassination of his son
b) Robbery of the Temple
c) Burning of Rome
d) None of the above

695. What activity led many early Christians into martyrdom?

a) Public preaching
b) Praying
c) Singing
d) None of the above

696. Which Roman emperor organized the last major persecution of Christians?

a) Nero
b) Caligula
c) Marcus Aurelius
d) Diocletian

697. What was the main reason for persecuting early Christians?

a) Refusal to worship Roman pagan gods
b) Refusal to pay taxes
c) Preaching of love
d) Attempted assassinations of the emperor

698. In what city did Emperor Valerian launch his brutal campaign against Christianity?
   a) Athens
   b) Rome
   c) Antioch
   d) Corinth

699. What was the name of the edict that made Christianity legal in the Roman Empire in 313 CE?
   a) Edict of Rome
   b) Edict of Jerusalem
   c) Edict of Milan
   d) Edict of Ravenna

700. What type of punishment did Emperor Decius order for anyone found practicing Christianity?
   a) Fines
   b) Torture
   c) Death
   d) Exile

701. Which book contains a chapter on the founding of the Church of Antioch?
   a) Acts
   b) Luke
   c) Revelation
   d) John

702. What practice became mandatory for Roman citizens in 250 CE with an edict issued by emperor Decius?
a) Having the statue of the emperor in every city
b) Public sacrifice
c) Worship of Zeus
d) None of the above

703. Which book in the Bible reports on how Stephen, an early Christian martyr, faced his accusers with courage and faith?
a) Acts
b) Genesis
c) Revelation
d) Romans

704. Which emperor issued an edict that required the citizens of the empire to sacrifice to the gods?
a) Constantine
b) Augustus
c) Decius
d) Trajan

705. According to the Bible, what did Paul and Silas do when they were thrown into prison for preaching Christianity?
a) Prayed
b) Fought
c) Cursed
d) None of the above

706. What type of punishment did Emperor Valerian order for anyone found practicing Christianity?

a) Banishment
b) Death
c) Fines
d) None of the above

707. During which period in history was Christian persecution at its worst?

a) The early Roman Empire
b) The Middle Ages
c) The Renaissance
d) The Enlightenment

708. Which Roman Emperor made Christianity legal throughout Rome in 313 CE?

a) Octavian Julius Caesar
b) Constantine
c) Tiberius
d) Nero

EXPANSION OF THE GOSPEL

In this chapter, we will explore questions that focus on Jesus' teachings about salvation through faith, grace, and love and the people who helped spread those messages. We'll look at questions like what does "gospel" refer to and who is credited with writing most of what we know about the gospel. Let's get started by diving into our first question.

709. What does the term "gospel" refer to?
a) Jesus' teachings in the writings of Matthew, Mark, Luke, and John
b) The four books of the New Testament that talk about Jesus' life and ministry
c) The message of salvation proclaimed by Jesus Christ
d) All of the above

710. What book in the Bible describes Philip preaching to an Ethiopian eunuch?
a) Acts
b) John
c) Galatians
d) Romans

711. What is the last passage about in the Book of Matthew?
a) The Ascension
b) The Great Commission
c) The Resurrection
d) None of the above

712. Acts of the Apostles is the continuation of which Evangelical gospel?
a) Matthew
b) Mark
c) Luke
d) John

713. Who was the first person to preach the gospel outside of Jerusalem?
a) Philip
b) Peter
c) James
d) Paul

714. Which of the gospels contain passages about the Great Commission?
a) Only Matthew
b) Matthew and Luke
c) Matthew, Luke, and Mark
d) Matthew, Mark, Luke, and John

715. What does the final chapter of the Gospel of Mark talk about?
a) The Ascension
b) The Resurrection
c) The Pentecost
d) None of the above

716. After Acts Chapter 8, who does not appear again in any further evangelistic efforts recorded in the Bible?
a) John
b) Matthew
c) Peter
d) Phillip

717. What did Jesus tell his disciples to preach to all nations?
a) The Ten Commandments
b) His death and resurrection
c) His miracles
d) All of the above

718. Which two books make up more than a fourth of the entire New Testament?
a) Mark and Matthew
b) Luke and Acts
c) Acts and Mark
d) Matthew and John

719. According to tradition, who wrote the Gospel of Mark?
a) Matthew
b) Luke
c) Paul
d) John Mark

720. In what language was the Gospel of Matthew written?
a) Hebrew
b) Greek
c) Latin
d) Aramaic

721. What is God identified with in the opening chapter of the Gospel of John?

a) Jesus
b) Love
c) The Word
d) Everything

722. How many Gospels are there in the New Testament?

a) One
b) Two
c) Three
d) Four

723. Which two books of the Bible contain most of Jesus' parables?

a) Mark and Luke
b) Matthew and Luke
c) Acts and Ephesians
d) Romans and Corinthians

724. Which canonical gospel is the shortest?

a) Luke
b) Mark
c) Matthew
d) John

725. Where is it recorded that Paul preached on Mars Hill in Athens?

a) Acts
b) Ephesians
c) Romans
d) Galatians

726. According to tradition, who wrote the Gospel of John?

a) Matthew
b) Luke
c) Paul
d) John

727. What is the last passage about in the Gospel of John?

a) Doubting Thomas
b) Reinstation of Peter
c) Jesus' Ascension
d) None of the above

728. Who wrote about Jesus' birth, ministry, death, resurrection, and instruction to his followers?

a) John
b) Mark
c) Matthew
d) All of the above

729. What is the source of power that Jesus promised to his followers?

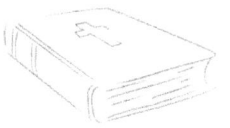

a) The Holy Spirit
b) Prayer
c) His teachings
d) Their faith

730. Which one of these authors is the single largest contributor to the New Testament?
a) Luke
b) Mark
c) Matthew
d) John

731. According to Acts 8:26-27, where was Philip the apostle sent to by an angel?
a) Egypt
b) Syria
c) Ethiopia
d) Armenia

Bible Trivia

THE SECOND COMING OF JESUS

While much about Jesus' return remains shrouded in mystery, certain aspects can be found in the scripture. The Bible reveals many details regarding this momentous event, such as what it is called and what signs indicate when he may come again. So, buckle up as we explore the topic of Jesus' Second Coming!

732. What is another name for the Second Coming of Jesus?

a) The Rapture
b) Armageddon
c) The Parousia
d) The Great Tribulation

733. In what part of the Bible do we find a description of Jesus' return to earth?

a) Old Testament
b) New Testament
c) Apocrypha
d) Pseudepigrapha

734. Which book in the Bible provides a detailed account of Jesus' second coming?

a) Revelation
b) Matthew
c) Genesis
d) John

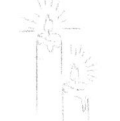

735. According to scripture, what will happen before Jesus returns?

a) Judgment Day
b) Rapture
c) One-thousand-year reign
d) All of the above

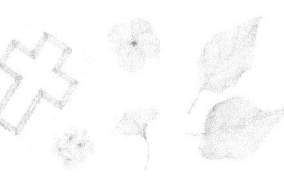

736. In which of these passages from the scripture is the second coming of Jesus prophesized?

a) Acts 1:10–11
b) John 3:16
c) Luke 8:43–48
d) None of the above

737. What are some signs that indicate when Christ's return might occur according to scripture?

a) Natural disasters
b) Signs in heaven
c) Wars and rumors of war
d) All of the above

738. According to scripture, what will be the result of Jesus' return?

a) Victory over death
b) Creation of a new heaven
c) Destruction of all evil
d) All of the above

739. What did Paul tell the Thessalonians regarding Christ's Second Coming?

a) Not to believe that Christ had already come again unless the rebellion had occurred
b) He may not return at all.
c) It is impossible to know when he will come.
d) None of the above

740. According to scripture, what is the purpose of Christ's return?
a) To punish the wicked
b) To bring peace on earth
c) To gather his people into paradise
d) All of the above

741. According to scripture, who is blessed because of Christ's return?
a) Believers in him
b) Evil people
c) Animals
d) Everyone on earth

742. At what time will Jesus come again, according to scripture?
a) It is not stated.
b) Noon
c) Midnight
d) Dawn

743. In addition to the Book of Revelation, which synoptic gospels mention the Second Coming of Christ?
a) Matthew and Mark
b) Mark and Luke
c) Luke and Matthew
d) All three of them

Bible Trivia

THE MILLENNIUM

The Millennium is described as Jesus' reign on earth. Answer questions about this foretold rule, including which book talks about it and how long Jesus will remain a ruler.

744. What is the name of the book in the Bible that talks about the Millennium?

a) Genesis
b) Revelation
c) Exodus
d) Numbers

745. How long would Jesus reign on earth during the Millennium?

a) One thousand years
b) Two thousand years
c) Three thousand years
d) Forever

746. What does the word "millennium" mean?

a) Middle age
b) One thousand years
c) End times
d) A new beginning

747. In what chapter of Revelation is Satan bound and chained for one thousand years?

a) Chapter 11
b) Chapter 12
c) Chapter 13
d) Chapter 20

748. According to some interpretations, who are the first to be resurrected to reign with Christ during the Millennium?
   a) Martyrs
   b) The saints
   c) The women and children
   d) None of the above

749. Who is said to one day reign with Jesus on earth during the Millennium?
   a) The saints
   b) All believers
   c) Angels
   d) Animals

750. What will be done to evil people who survive all tribulations and wars before entering these one thousand years?
   a) They will receive new bodies.
   b) They will suffer for their deeds.
   c) They will instantly die.
   d) They will not have to face any judgment.

751. What does Isaiah describe as being part of life during Christ's rule on earth?
   a) The Kingdom of Israel
   b) A new beginning
   c) Sadness
   d) Peace

752. What will happen to the animal kingdom during the Millennium?

a) They will all be destroyed.
b) They will only exist in heaven.
c) They are not mentioned at all.
d) They will live peacefully alongside humans.

753. According to Revelation, what event marks the start of the Millennium?

a) Jesus' return
b) The resurrection of the dead
c) Satan's binding in hell
d) The cleansing of the earth

754. What do scholars typically refer to as the Rapture?

a) The resurrection of dead Christians and their rise to the skies
b) The cleansing of the earth
c) Satan's binding in hell
d) Jesus' return

755. What is the purpose of the Millennium?

a) To get rid of the earth
b) To punish sinners
c) To reward saints
d) To restore God's kingdom on earth

756. In what book does Isaiah talk about peace and prosperity that comes during Christ's reign on earth?

a) Genesis
b) Exodus
c) Isaiah
d) Revelation

757. What will happen to Satan after the Millennium is complete?

a) He will be set free.
b) He will be destroyed.
c) He will remain bound in hell.
d) None of the above.

758. What will happen to the earth during the Millennium, according to Revelation?

a) It will be purified.
b) It will be destroyed.
c) It will remain unchanged.
d) None of the above.

FINAL JUDGMENT

The Day of Judgment is a concept that has been spoken about in many religious traditions. It speaks of a day when all will be judged for their actions during life. This section looks at the Final Judgment and poses questions such as who will be judged, what criteria they are being judged on, and how judgment is carried out.

759. According to the Bible, who will be judged on the Day of Judgment?
a) Believers in Jesus Christ
b) Unbelievers in Jesus Christ
c) Those with good moral character
d) All people

760. What is the primary criterion for judgment according to Matthew 25:31-46?
a) Faithfulness and loyalty toward others
b) The amount of time spent in prayer
c) Good works done during life
d) None of the above

761. How many books are opened at the Final Judgment as described in Revelation 20:12?
a) Five
b) Two
c) Three
d) Four

762. Which book mentioned in Revelation contains an account of all people's deeds during their lifetime?
a) The Book of Life
b) The Book of the Dead
c) The First Book
d) It is not mentioned.

763. What sin, according to 1 Corinthians 6, is a sin against one's own body?
a) Sexual immorality
b) Breaking the fast
c) Idolatry
d) Worship of Satan

764. According to Revelation 20:15, who will be thrown into hell after being judged?
a) Those with no faith in Jesus Christ
b) Those whose names are not written in the Book of Life.
c) All sinners
d) All believers

765. What color is the throne that is described in Revelation 20:11?
a) Red
b) Black
c) White
d) Gold

766. What is the lake of fire described in Revelation 20:14-15?
a) A place for God's judgment
b) The second death
c) Everlasting life
d) An image to scare sinners into repentance

767. Who presides over the Final Judgment as mentioned in John 5:22-23?

a) Jesus Christ
b) Satan
c) Gabriel
d) Michael

768. On what basis does Jesus judge people according to Hebrews 4:13?

a) By their faith and loyalty toward him
b) By assessing their hearts and minds
c) By determining the number of good deeds done during their life
d) Through an examination of all they have said or done throughout their lifetime

769. To whom does 1 Peter 4:5 compare the people who have sinned?

a) Satan
b) Gentiles
c) Pagans
d) None of the above

770. In which chapter does Revelation describe the opening books at the Final Judgment?

a) Chapter 10
b) Chapter 13
c) Chapter 15
d) Chapter 20

771. In Matthew 25, what does Jesus say about those thrown out on Judgment Day?
a) *They are cursed forever.*
b) *They shall find peace.*
c) *There is no hope of redemption.*
d) *Their punishment is everlasting.*

772. In what chapter of Revelation is the lake of fire described?
a) *Chapter 19*
b) *Chapter 20*
c) *Chapter 22*
d) *Chapter 23*

Bible Trivia

HEAVEN

The Bible touches on heaven in many different books. These questions will test your knowledge of what has been written, such as what kind of fruit grows on its trees and the name of the heavenly city's great white throne. Don't forget you can find the answers at the end of the book!

773. What is the place of eternal bliss where God and his angels dwell?
a) Heaven
b) The Garden of Eden
c) Hell
d) Purgatory

774. How many angels guard God's throne in heaven?
a) Two hundred million
b) Three thousand
c) Fourteen
d) It is not specified.

775. In which book does Jesus say, "I go to prepare a place for you?"
a) John
b) Revelation
c) Luke
d) Matthew

776. What is the name of the throne where God sits in judgment according to Revelation 20:11?
a) The Throne of Grace
b) The Mercy Seat
c) The Throne of Justice
d) The Great White Throne

777. According to Isaiah 25:8, what happens when people who have suffered on earth are brought into God's presence in heaven?
   a) They will experience no more sorrow.
   b) They will receive their rewards.
   c) They will be given new bodies.
   d) None of the above.

778. In what book does it say that the streets of heaven are made from gold and its gates from pearls?
   a) Psalms
   b) Proverbs
   c) Matthew
   d) Revelation

779. What will never be needed in heaven?
   a) Money
   b) Food
   c) Jobs
   d) All of the above

780. In what book does it say that God's throne is surrounded by Seraphim?
   a) Job
   b) Isaiah
   c) Psalms
   d) Jeremiah

781. According to Romans 8:18, what can believers look forward to when they enter heaven?

a) A new life
b) No more suffering
c) Unending pleasure
d) None of the above

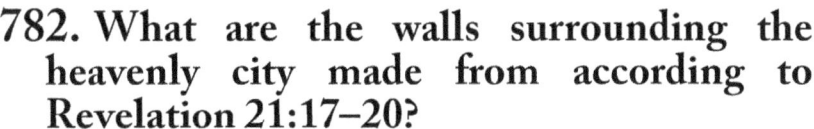

782. What are the walls surrounding the heavenly city made from according to Revelation 21:17–20?

a) Jasper
b) Diamonds
c) Rubies
d) Pearls

783. According to Revelation 4:3, how many eyes does each of the four living creatures have in heaven?

a) Four
b) Two
c) Six
d) It is not specified.

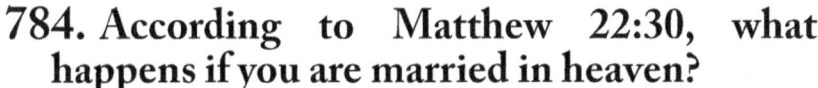

784. According to Matthew 22:30, what happens if you are married in heaven?

a) You will remain together for eternity.
b) You will be separated.
c) You will have different partners.
d) You cannot marry in heaven.

785. In what book does it say that God's dwelling place is above the heavens?
a) Genesis
b) Proverbs
c) Isaiah
d) Exodus

786. What kind of tree stands by the river according to Revelation 22:2?
a) Cedar tree
b) Oak tree
c) Apple tree
d) Tree of life

787. Who will accompany Jesus when he descends from heaven?
a) God
b) Peter
c) Angels
d) Adam

788. What type of fruit grows on the trees lining the heavenly city's streets according to Revelation 22:2?
a) Many different types of fruit
b) Grapes
c) Apples
d) The fruits of life

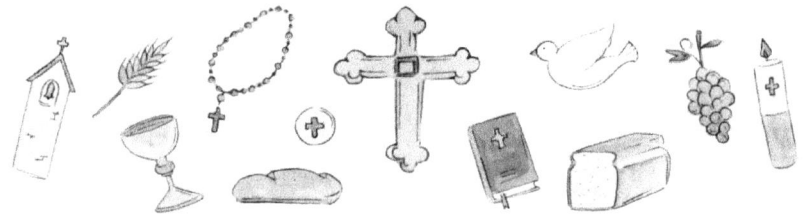

789. In what book does it say that heaven is God's throne?

a) Psalms
b) Matthew
c) Isaiah
d) All of the above

790. Which stone out of these is not mentioned in Ezekiel 28:13-14?

a) Lapis
b) Sapphire
c) Emerald
d) Topaz

791. In what book does it say that there is no night in heaven?

a) Isaiah
b) Revelation
c) John
d) Matthew

792. How many gates does heaven have according to Revelation 21:21?

a) Five
b) Twelve
c) Seven
d) Twenty-two

Bible Trivia

ANGELS

Angels are mysterious and powerful beings mentioned in both the Old and New Testaments. In traditional Christian art, angels have been depicted with two or four wings, but how many do they usually have? What is the name of the fallen angel who rebelled against God's authority? This chapter will ask these questions and more!

793. How many wings do angels usually have in traditional Christian art?

   a) Four
   b) Two
   c) Six
   d) Eight

794. How many wings are angels depicted with in the Bible?

   a) Two
   b) Four
   c) Twenty
   d) It is never stated.

795. What is the name of the fallen angel who rebelled against God's authority?

   a) Lucifer
   b) Satan
   c) Zagan
   d) Beelzebub

796. Who was Daniel guided by during his time in the Babylonian captivity?

   a) Archangel Gabriel
   b) Angel Jophiel
   c) Cherubim
   d) Seraphim

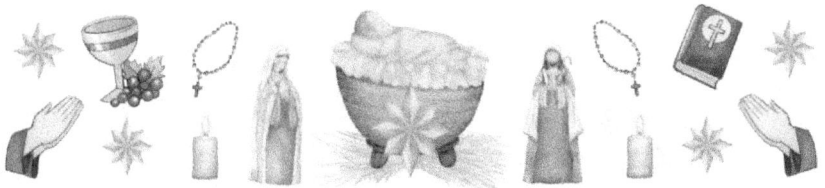

797. Which book of the Bible mentions an angel named Abaddon?
a) Ezekiel
b) Revelation
c) Daniel
d) Genesis

798. How many archangels are mentioned in the Bible?
a) Two
b) Three
c) Six
d) Eight

799. What did God appoint Michael to be the prince of?
a) Heaven
b) Hell
c) Earth
d) Israel

800. Who was sent by God to defeat 185,000 Assyrian soldiers in one night?
a) Archangel Gabriel
b) Angel Jophiel
c) Abaddon
d) It is not specified.

801. In what book does an angel appear to Gideon and announce his destiny as a great leader for Israel?

a) Numbers
b) Judges
c) Exodus
d) Deuteronomy

802. According to the Book of Revelation, which angel is given authority over the bottomless pit?

a) Seraphim
b) Beelzebub
c) Abaddon
d) Lucifer

803. In which book can you find angels being summoned by the sound of a trumpet?

a) Numbers
b) Isaiah
c) Ezekiel
d) Revelation

804. Who was sent by God to destroy Sodom and Gomorrah, two cities filled with wickedness?

a) Two angels
b) Archangel Gabriel
c) An army of Israelites
d) None of the above

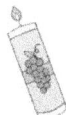     

805. How many angels were present at Jesus' tomb after his resurrection from the dead?
a) Two
b) Four
c) Six
d) Eight

806. In what book does an angel appear in Jacob's dream on his journey back home from Mesopotamia?
a) Genesis
b) Exodus
c) Leviticus
d) Deuteronomy

807. Who was the angel who fought against Satan to defend Moses' body?
a) Abaddon
b) Uriel
c) Michael
d) Raphael

808. What did the archangel command when he disputed with Satan over possession of Moses' body?
a) "Be gone!"
b) "God will not forget."
c) "The Lord rebuke you!"
d) "You will be punished!"

809. To whom did the angel appear in Genesis 22:11-15?

a) Hagar
b) Moses
c) Jacob
d) Abraham

810. In what book do angels announce good news to shepherds outside Bethlehem?

a) Numbers
b) Judges
c) Luke
d) Deuteronomy

811. How many angels guarded Eden after Adam and Eve's expulsion from it, according to Genesis 3:24?

a) Two
b) Four
c) Six
d) It is not specified.

812. In which book can you find an angel rescuing Lot's wife, who had turned into a pillar of salt for disobeying orders?

a) Ezekiel
b) Isaiah
c) Matthew
d) Genesis

813. What task did an angel perform for Elijah in 1 Kings 19:5-7?
a) Brought him food and drink
b) Set fire to his enemies
c) Helped him escape danger
d) It is not specified.

814. In what book does an angel appear to Joshua at Jericho?
a) Numbers
b) Judges
c) Exodus
d) Joshua

815. Who is believed to be the most powerful of all angels, according to Jewish mythology?
a) Archangel Gabriel
b) Angel Jophiel
c) Metatron
d) Satan

816. How did Zechariah feel when an angel appeared before him while offering incense at the altar of incense?
a) He was excited.
b) He was afraid.
c) He did not react.
d) None of the above.

817. How many angels are named in the New Testament?
  a) Two
  b) Four
  c) Three
  d) Eight

818. What type of creatures did Ezekiel see in his vision that he described as having four faces and four wings?
  a) Cherubim
  b) Seraphim
  c) Angels
  d) Beasts

Bible Trivia

DEMONS AND MONSTERS

For centuries, these otherworldly creatures have captured our imaginations with stories of temptation and terror. From the story of Jesus in the wilderness to Jewish folklore about dybbuks, we'll explore dark forces believed to exist in scripture and in the Abrahamic traditions. We will step outside of the Bible for a few of these questions, but we hope you leave this section learning something new.

819. According to scripture, what happened when Jesus commanded a group of demons to leave their human hosts and enter a herd of pigs?

a) The pigs ran down a cliff into the sea.
b) They caused an earthquake that destroyed part of a town.
c) The pigs became violent and attacked each other.
d) The demons went peacefully, and no harm came to anyone.

820. In Jewish folklore, what are dybbukim believed to be?

a) Malicious disembodied human spirit
b) Demons inhabiting humans
c) Demons who bring misfortune
d) Demons who cause disease

821. In the Book of Job, what is Behemoth described as?

a) A giant sea creature
b) A powerful storm
c) A great dragon
d) An elephant-like beast

822. According to some stories in Jewish folklore, what do demons feed on?

a) Souls
b) Blood
c) Dirt
d) There isn't a set belief for this.

823. In Jewish folklore, what is Lilin said to do?

a) Attack men
b) Create chaos
c) Steal children
d) Possess humans

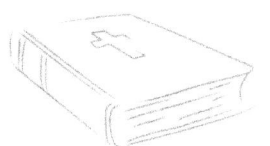

824. According to some Christian traditions, what is the name of the demon who tempts people with lust?

a) Incubus
b) Behemoth
c) Beelzebul
d) Mammoth

825. In Jewish folklore, what is Samael known as?

a) A nice demon
b) The king of an evil realm
c) The archangel of death
d) A powerful fallen angel

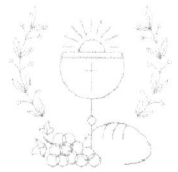

826. What did Jesus tell the Gerasene possessed man to do when he was healed?

a) "Go and tell the people what the Lord has done for you."
b) "Preach the gospel."
c) "Pray for forgiveness."
d) "Follow me."

827. In Jewish folklore, what are shedim believed to be?

a) Fierce warriors
b) Wild beasts
c) Evil spirits or demons
d) Fallen angels

828. According to scripture, how many demons did Jesus cast out of Mary Magdalene?

a) Two
b) Five
c) Seven
d) It is not specified.

829. According to Christian tradition, who is Belial usually associated with?

a) God
b) Satan
c) Angels
d) None of the above

830. Why did Jesus help the Syrophoenician woman's daughter who was possessed?

a) It's not his mission.
b) He helped her because of her faith.
c) She should cast them out herself.
d) He would send his disciples to help her.

831. According to some Christian traditions, what is the name of a group of seven powerful demons?

a) The Fallen Ones
b) The Seven Seraphim
c) The Seven Princes of Hell
d) The Seven Archangels

832. Who was with Jesus when he cast out the demons from the Gerasene demoniac?

a) The disciples
b) A crowd of onlookers
c) His mother Mary
d) None of the above

833. In Jewish folklore, what are shedim believed to do?

a) Cause sickness
b) Grant wishes
c) Steal children
d) None of the above

834. What did Jesus command an unclean spirit when he encountered it in a synagogue?

a) "Go and sin no more."
b) "Come out of him!"
c) "Follow me."
d) "Pray for forgiveness."

835. According to some Christian traditions, who is the prince of demons?

a) Baalzebub
b) Zechariah
c) Belphegor
d) Satan

Bible Trivia

SATAN

Satan is a figure renowned in the Christian tradition and in pop culture. He is often referred to by different names. In this chapter, we will explore what the scripture tells us about Satan and how he has been represented in the Bible.

836. What does the Bible refer to Satan as?
a) The tempter
b) The evil one
c) A roaring lion
d) All of the above

837. In which book is Satan mentioned (or alluded to) for the first time?
a) Genesis
b) Exodus
c) Job
d) Deuteronomy

838. In what book in the Bible can we find an account where Jesus is tempted by Satan?
a) Matthew
b) Acts
c) Revelation
d) John

839. What does Ephesians 6:11 tell us to put on against the schemes of the devil?
a) Clothes
b) Shields and swords
c) Armor of God
d) Money

840. Which chapter in Job tells how Satan got permission from God to test Job's faithfulness?
a) Chapter 1
b) Chapter 4
c) Chapter 7
d) Chapter 10

841. How did Satan try to persuade Jesus to turn stones into bread?
a) By offering money
b) By appealing to his hunger
c) By using force
d) By questioning his trust in God's power

842. Who is referred to as the "father of lies" in John 8:44?
a) Adam
b) Abraham
c) The devil
d) Demons

843. According to Isaiah 14:12-14, what name did Satan have before his fall from grace?
a) Lucifer
b) Abaddon
c) Belial
d) Beelzebub

844. What is the meaning of the word "Satan?"

a) Adversary
b) Destroyer
c) Prince
d) Deceiver

845. Which verse tells us that we should resist Satan when he tempts us?

a) James 4:7
b) Jude 1:9
c) Ephesians 6:11
d) Peter 5:8

846. How did Jesus refer to Satan in Matthew 4:3-4?

a) A very evil man
b) An adversary
c) A tempter
d) A thief

847. In 1 Peter 5:8, how should we resist Satan's temptations?

a) With prayer and fasting
b) By fleeing from him
c) With faith and patience
d) By being alert and of sober mind

848. What did Job's wife tell him to do when he was suffering from Satan's attacks?

a) Bless God
b) Curse God
c) Ignore it
d) Accept his punishment

849. Who is said to be "the accuser of our brothers and sisters, who accuses them before our God day and night" in Revelation 12:9-10?

a) The Beast
b) Antichrist
c) Satan
d) None of the above

850. Who is said to have bound and chained the dragon (Satan) for a thousand years, according to Revelation 20?

a) Michael
b) Jesus Christ
c) Gabriel
d) It is not specified.

CONCLUSION

This trivia book of the Bible has explored a wide range of topics, from creation to Judgment Day.

You have answered questions on how God created the heavens and earth, formed Adam and Eve in his image, and provided them with the Garden of Eden as their home.

After sin entered the world, we went on a trivia journey through Noah's flood, Abraham's family line, Joseph's story, Moses leading the Israelites to freedom, and Moses receiving the Ten Commandments at Mount Sinai.

From Elijah confronting wicked kings to Esther saving her people from destruction, you have answered dozens of questions about courage and faithfulness in times of trial while being reminded throughout that God is always faithful no matter what lies ahead.

Bible Trivia has been filled with lessons about faith in God's promises, no matter what our circumstances may be. Through the Bible, we can see how he is always faithful to us, even if it takes centuries or millennia for us to see his plan unfold.

ANSWER KEY

CREATION OF THE HEAVENS AND THE EARTH

1. a. Six
2. a. Separation of light from darkness
3. b. Land and plants
4. a. Water and sky animals
5. d. Sixth day
6. a. God
7. c. He created the sky
8. a. One
9. a. Create the sun, moon, and stars
10. b. Good

CREATION OF ADAM AND EVE

11. d. Genesis
12. b. Dust of the ground
13. c. Adam
14. d. Eve
15. d. The rib of Adam
16. a. They were created in God's image
17. a. The Garden of Eden
18. d. All of the above
19. a. One day
20. b. They were equals
21. d. All of the above
22. a. Adam

GARDEN OF EDEN

23. a. God
24. d. Tree of the knowledge of good and evil
25. b. Fruit from the forbidden tree
26. d. None of the above
27. c. Four
28. d. Unknown
29. a. Tree of Knowledge
30. d. Not specified
31. a. Adam and Eve
32. a. Genesis
33. d. Cherubim
34. a. Place of pleasure

SIN AND EXPULSION FROM THE GARDEN OF EDEN

35. d. Do not eat or touch it.
36. a. Through disobedience to God's commandment
37. c. A serpent
38. c. He curses it into being forced to crawl on its belly and eat dust.
39. a. Coats of skins
40. a. Unspecified
41. c. He placed angels at its entrance.
42. d. Unknown
43. a. They were ashamed
44. d. All of the above
45. a. Forever

46. a. They became mortal

ADAM AND EVE'S LINEAGE

47. b. Three
48. b. Enoch
49. d. Irad
50. b. Terah
51. b. Abraham and Sarah
52. d. Mahalath
53. a. Landowner
54. b. Nineteen
55. c. Bathsheba
56. d. All of the above
57. a. Joseph
58. a. Elizabeth and Zechariah
59. c. Six
60. a. Laban
61. c. Jacob
62. c. Ham
63. b. Michal
64. a. Ahaz

NOAH AND THE GREAT FLOOD

65. b. Forty days and forty nights
66. d. None of the above
67. d. God
68. b. Two
69. d. Gopher wood
70. b. Seven days
71. c. To sacrifice as an offering to God
72. a. Repent your sins or be destroyed.
73. a. Build an altar to God
74. b. Raven
75. a. Mount Ararat
76. b. Became a farmer
77. a. 5000 BCE
78. a. To never send such punishment again
79. a. Family members

TOWER OF BABEL

80. c. Shinar
81. c. To make a name for themselves by reaching heaven
82. d. None of the above
83. a. God confused people's language so they spoke different languages.
84. d. Unspecified.
85. c. He disapproved.
86. d. God
87. b. Genesis
88. b. He destroyed it.
89. d. God

ABRAHAM AND HIS FAMILY

90. a. Shepherd
91. b. Hagar
92. a. One
93. a. "God will provide the lamb for his own sacrifice."
94. c. Send them away.
95. b. That he would be Abraham's shield and protector
96. d. He was king at the time that Abraham returned from battle victorious.
97. c. Ninety years old
98. d. Sarah
99. c. Canaan
100. c. Princess of nations
101. b. She laughed in disbelief.
102. c. All of the above
103. d. Seventy-five years old

104. b. Canaan
105. d. Arabs
106. a. A slave from Egypt
107. b. 85 years old
108. b. The wilderness of Paran
109. a. Twelve sons
110. a. An angel

ISAAC, ABRAHAM'S SON

111. a. Abimelech
112. a. Moriah
113. d. Abraham
114. a. Joyful laughter
115. b. Servants
116. a. Rebecca
117. b. Ten camels
118. c. God appeared in a dream.
119. a. One hundred years old
120. a. A cave in the wilderness of Machpelah
121. c. Ram
122. a. "Do not lay a hand on the boy."
123. d. "Now I know that you fear God."
124. a. The power and glory of God
125. a. Three days
126. b. Hebron

JACOB, ESAU, AND RACHEL

127. a. A bowl of stew
128. c. Jacob
129. d. God
130. b. To receive the family inheritance
131. a. She lied to Isaac about who was asking for the blessing.
132. b. Angels ascending and descending a ladder
133. c. Fourteen years
134. a. Rebecca and Jacob
135. a. He threatened to kill Jacob.
136. a. She advised him to flee to Laban.
137. b. Two wives
138. a. She denied it.
139. a. Egypt
140. b. The fathers of the twelve tribes of Israel

JOSEPH AND HIS JOURNEY

141. a. Jacob
142. b. They were jealous of Joseph.
143. c. Both A and B
144. c. Thirty years old
145. a. Egypt
146. b. Two
147. c. Traveled to Egypt
148. d. Joseph
149. d. Joseph himself
150. b. Two
151. a. Manasseh
152. a. In cisterns in different Egyptian cities
153. d. Eleven
154. a. Joseph
155. d. Ephraim

THE TEN PLAGUES OF EGYPT

156. c. Blood in the Nile River
157. a. Three days
158. b. Gnats or lice
159. d. Cattle
160. a. The Israelites
161. d. Darkness
162. d. None of the above

163. d. Death of all Egyptian firstborns
164. b. God
165. b. Passover
166. a. The newborn Hebrew daughters
167. c. God caused the wind to blow.
168. a. A lamb

THE EXODUS

169. a. Aaron
170. c. By drowning in the Red Sea after God parted it for Moses and his people
171. d. Moses
172. d. Moses (A is also acceptable)
173. b. After the burning bush experience
174. d. Bithiah
175. a. Forty years
176. b. He instructed Moses to divide it.
177. a. Eighty years old
178. a. 600,000
179. d. Moses
180. a. Manna and quail
181. b. A pillar of cloud and a pillar of smoke
182. c. A golden calf

THE TEN COMMANDMENTS

183. a. Moses
184. a. On stone tablets
185. a. Mount Sinai
186. d. Two
187. c. Do unto others as you would have them do unto you.
188. a. Stay loyal to God
189. d. All of the above
190. b. Building altars to God
191. a. Do not tell lies about others

THE JOURNEY TO THE PROMISED LAND

192. d. Joshua
193. c. Twelve
194. a. Twelve tribes
195. b. The Jordan River
196. c. Jericho
197. a. Seven days

THE JUDGES

198. a. Samuel
199. a. He attacked him with a knife hidden under his cloak.
200. a. He wanted to punish its people for not supporting him.
201. d. To sacrifice whatever came out first when he returned home
202. b. They had sixty sons and daughters.
203. d. Midianites
204. a. It was an oxgoad.
205. a. Prophet
206. d. He turns their swords against each other.
207. d. His family
208. b. He was seized by the Philistines
209. a. Samson

THE KINGDOM OF ISRAEL

210. b. David
211. a. Saul

212. c. 11th century BCE
213. a. Solomon
214. d. Seven
215. a. Nehemiah
216. b. Solomon
217. b. Othniel
218. d. Ish-bosheth
219. c. Kish
220. a. Solomon
221. d. Jeroboam
222. a. 120 years
223. c. Samuel
224. c. David
225. b. Samuel
226. a. Battle of Mount Gilboa
227. c. Absalom
228. d. None of the above
229. b. Hazor
230. a. Spear
231. a. Michal
232. c. Valley of Elah
233. a. Rehoboam
234. c. Seven hundred wives
235. b. Solomon
236. c. Forty years
237. b. Hebron

GOLIATH AND DAVID

238. d. Saph
239. b. Seven
240. d. Slingshot
241. c. Samuel
242. a. A little more than six cubits
243. c. The Philistines
244. b. He brought it to Jerusalem.
245. d. Not stated
246. d. His daughter
247. d. His everyday clothes
248. b. Bethlehem
249. b. He kept it.
250. a. Shepherd
251. c. Harp
252. a. One day
253. d. Food
254. c. Five
255. b. His armor

SOLOMON AND HIS REIGN

256. a. Nathan
257. a. Seventy years old
258. b. The baby should be split in half.
259. b. It went home with its rightful mother.
260. b. Hiram
261. d. All of the above
262. a. He worshiped other gods.
263. d. Ahijah
264. a. The Temple
265. b. Forty years
266. d. All of the above
267. d. Solomon
268. a. None of the above
269. a. 967 BC
270. c. The queen of Sheba
271. a. His wisdom
272. c. The Second Temple
273. d. Wisdom

REHOBOAM AND THE DIVIDED KINGDOM

274. a. Refused their request for lighter taxes
275. d. Israel
276. a. Shemaiah
277. a. Jeroboam
278. b. Idols
279. d. The elders
280. a. Abijah
281. a. Abijah

282. c. A little over twenty years
283. d. Twelve
284. a. Asa
285. c. He would grant him an enduring dynasty.
286. c. Worshiping idols
287. a. Ahijah

ELIJAH

288. d. It is not established.
289. d. He called down fire from heaven.
290. b. Elisha
291. b. Beersheba
292. c. He was given instructions to go back and anoint Hazael as king.
293. a. Anointed Elisha to be his successor
294. d. None of the above
295. d. The widow of Zarephath
296. d. In a whirlwind
297. c. Inherit a double portion of his spirit
298. b. Mount Carmel
299. d. It was picked up by Elisha
300. b. Moses

ELISHA

301. b. Purifying a town's water
302. b. The King of Aram
303. c. He and his descendants were cursed with leprosy.
304. a. Olive oil
305. c. One hundred
306. a. The Jordan River
307. b. Forty-two
308. a. He called down a curse in the name of God.
309. d. The Shunammite Woman

310. a. Salt
311. d. Elisha
312. d. It is not specified.
313. a. He told Naaman to bathe in the Jordan River seven times.
314. d. The Shunammite Woman

KINGS OF JUDAH AND ISRAEL

315. a. Jehu
316. b. Elisha
317. b. Athaliah
318. a. Twenty
319. b. Hezekiah
320. a. Joash
321. a. Hezekiah
322. a. Nadab
323. d. Israel
324. c. Joash
325. a. Omri
326. a. Zedekiah
327. d. Babylonian Empire
328. a. Zechariah
329. d. Amos
330. d. Jehoram
331. b. Hezekiah
332. b. Jezebel

PROPHETS OF THE OLD TESTAMENT

333. a. Jeremiah
334. a. Jeremiah
335. d. All of the above
336. d. All of the above
337. b. Jeremiah
338. b. Jonah
339. b. The end of the Babylonian captivity
340. d. Samuel
341. b. Israel

342. d. All of the above

THE BABYLONIAN CAPTIVITY

343. a. Nebuchadnezzar II
344. a. Seventy years
345. b. Jeremiah
346. c. Babylon's war with Persia
347. d. As a punishment for disobeying God (B is also acceptable)
348. b. The Book of Daniel
349. b. Cyrus the Great
350. b. Jehoiachin
351. b. A vision given to Daniel
352. d. The Book of Ezra
353. b. He was Jehoiachin's uncle
354. a. 538 BCE
355. d. Gedaliah
356. d. Nehemiah
357. b. Zerubbabel
358. d. More than forty years
359. b. King Cyrus helped by providing funds.
360. d. Ezra
361. b. Joshua
362. a. More than forty thousand
363. a. period when the people were allowed to return home and some of their debts were forgiven

ESTHER AND THE PURIM STORY

364. a. Stand up for her people and save them from destruction
365. b. 5th century BCE
366. a. Two times
367. a. Chief advisor to the king
368. b. Wine
369. b. To celebrate the victory of Mordecai and Esther
370. a. Vashti
371. a. Fast and pray
372. b. It is one of only two books in the Bible that don't mention God.
373. c. Esther
374. b. Bowing down before him
375. b. An annual celebration in honor of Queen Esther

BIRTH OF JOHN THE BAPTIST

376. a. Zechariah
377. b. Joy
378. a. They were advanced in age.
379. a. He was struck dumb.
380. c. Nine months
381. a. An angel
382. c. Six months
383. b. Cousin
384. b. She stayed with her cousin for three months
385. a. They praised God.
386. a. He praised God.

THE ANNUNCIATION TO THE BLESSED VIRGIN

387. b. The Gospel of Luke
388. a. An angel
389. b. Emmanuel
390. a. Joseph
391. c. "Do not be afraid, for you have found favor with God."
392. a. In Nazareth
393. a. Gabriel
394. b. He wanted to divorce her.
395. a. He will be great and will be called the Son of God.

396. c. The Feast of the Annunciation
397. d. She asked for further clarification.
398. c. It symbolizes obedience and faithfulness to God.
399. c. March 25th
400. b. "Blessed are you among women."
401. b. Mary and Gabriel

JESUS' BIRTH

402. a. Micah
403. c. Matthew and Luke
404. c. In a stable in Bethlehem
405. c. An angel told the shepherds nearby.
406. b. Christmas
407. a. The Star of Bethlehem
408. b. Three
409. a. King David
410. c. Swaddling bands
411. a. Frankincense, gold, and myrrh
412. d. King Herod
413. b. He had his circumcision ceremony.
414. a. To escape King Herod, who wanted to kill Jesus
415. b. Donkey
416. a. God with us
417. c. He moved to Nazareth.
418. b. Forty days old

BAPTISM OF JESUS

419. a. Jordan River
420. b. "This is my beloved Son."
421. a. John the Baptist and the Holy Spirit
422. b. Around thirty years old
423. c. To prove his divinity
424. c. The Spirit of God descended upon him.
425. a. It marked the beginning of his earthly mission.
426. a. "I need to be baptized by you, and do you come to me?"
427. a. It showed humility and obedience.
428. d. John the Baptist
429. a. Because he felt unworthy
430. b. To symbolically cleanse them from sin
431. d. John
432. a. "Behold, the Lamb of God!"
433. a. They were seeking forgiveness through confession and repentance.
434. d. All of the above.

MINISTRY AND MIRACLES OF JESUS

435. a. Turning water into wine
436. a. To preach and teach about God's kingdom
437. c. He reprimanded them.
438. b. "Your sins are forgiven."
439. c. Capernaum
440. d. Four
441. a. He paid his and Peter's tax with a four-drachma coin.
442. b. Cana
443. d. It demonstrated his glory and holy ability.
444. a. About five thousand
445. c. "Here truly is an Israelite in whom there is no deceit."
446. b. He told her that he did not condemn her.
447. a. How to receive eternal life

448. c. Four men
449. b. Because Jesus' house was full of his many followers
450. b. He is testing Jesus.
451. d. John
452. b. By multiplying bread and fish
453. c. He turned over their tables.
454. c. Ten
455. d. Jairus's daughter
456. b. He scolded them
457. c. Luke
458. c. A rich young man
459. a. We will be forgiven in return.
460. d. Love God with all your heart.
461. a. A blind man from Bethsaida
462. b. Belief in him
463. b. On a mountain near Capernaum
464. d. A Samaritan woman
465. a. Salvation has come to his home today.

TEMPTATION OF JESUS

466. b. "Man shall not live by bread alone, but by every word that proceeds from the mouth of God."
467. c. Three times
468. b. Angels
469. c. Power
470. c. Matthew
471. c. Forty days
472. c. Bread
473. a. Turn stones into bread
474. c. People should put their trust in God.
475. c. Galilee
476. d. All of the above

SERMON ON THE MOUNT

477. c. To provide instructions for how to live as God intended
478. d. It is not specified.
479. c. Near Galilee
480. a. Several days
481. a. The Beatitudes
482. c. Eight
483. c. Those who hunger and thirst after fame
484. d. Forgive them
485. a. They were amazed.
486. c. Righteous
487. b. Love their enemies.
488. c. To fulfill the law
489. a. His disciples
490. a. A sin
491. c. Seek revenge
492. c. An idiot or fool
493. d. It should be avoided.
494. d. Turn the other cheek

PARABLES OF JESUS

495. a. A moral lesson
496. d. The Parable of the Persistent Widow
497. a. The Prodigal Son
498. c. Lost Sheep and Coin
499. a. The consequences of a life lived without God
500. d. The Good Samaritan
501. d. To sow generously with no expectation of return
502. d. To warn against hoarding wealth for selfish reasons

503. a. To help those in need regardless of their background or beliefs
504. c. Great things come from small beginnings.
505. a. The Parable of the Ten Virgins
506. b. The Parable of the Talents
507. a. Forgiveness is essential if we wish to attain salvation.
508. b. The Parable of the Talents
509. c. Everyone deserves second chances.
510. b. Good Samaritan

JESUS' ENTRY INTO JERUSALEM

511. a. The Triumphal Entry
512. c. Donkey
513. b. Palm branches
514. d. The people of Israel
515. a. Bethany
516. d. All four Gospels
517. c. The disciples
518. a. "Hosanna!"
519. d. Five
520. a. Mary Magdalene
521. a. He wept.
522. b. Bethany
523. d. All of the above
524. a. Passover
525. d. To celebrate Passover

THE LAST SUPPER

526. b. Lamb, unleavened bread, and bitter herbs
527. a. In a room on Mount Zion
528. a. Jesus and all twelve of his disciples
529. a. He left early.
530. c. Blessed it
531. b. Judas Iscariot
532. d. Four
533. d. On Thursday
534. d. To always love one another
535. a. On Jesus' bosom
536. b. As the betrayer
537. b. Eucharist
538. b. A loaf of bread
539. a. Mary Magdalene
540. a. To remember God's protection of his people
541. d. Not to worry about him

THE CRUCIFIXION OF JESUS

542. b. Pontius Pilate
543. c. Three times
544. a. Friday
545. d. All of the above
546. b. Three times
547. d. Purple
548. b. Joseph of Arimathea
549. a. With being thieves
550. b. Six hours
551. d. "Father, into thy hands I commend my spirit."
552. c. Jesus' mother, Mary
553. d. Vinegar
554. a. King of the Jews
555. d. All of them
556. a. A crown of thorns
557. a. The centurion
558. b. Mary Magdalene
559. b. Divided them among themselves

RESURRECTION OF JESUS

560. a. Three days
561. a. "Peace be with you."
562. c. At Jesus' tomb

563. d. After he had met the other disciples first
564. b. Two
565. b. "I have seen him."
566. a. An angel
567. d. None of the above
568. a. Mary Magdalene
569. a. They were stupefied.
570. c. Nothing
571. a. Joseph of Arimathea
572. b. "Do not be afraid."
573. b. 33 CE
574. c. Doubt

ASCENSION OF JESUS

575. d. Ascended to heaven
576. b. Forty days
577. c. The Mount of Olives
578. b. Acts
579. d. Luke
580. c. Eleven
581. c. Judas
582. b. Jerusalem
583. d. They continued preaching.
584. c. It is not known.
585. b. At the right hand of God
586. d. Acts
587. d. "This same Jesus shall so come in like manner as ye have seen him go into heaven."
588. a. Angels
589. d. All of the above
590. d. All of the above

THE DAY OF PENTECOST

591. b. Fiftieth
592. d. The descent of the Holy Spirit
593. d. Ten days
594. c. Noises from heaven
595. a. Peter
596. a. Around three thousand people were saved from their sins.
597. a. Shavuot
598. d. They received the Holy Spirit.
599. a. Dove
600. a. Repent and be baptized.
601. a. Fire and wind
602. c. Luke
603. c. They preached in the name of God.
604. d. Luck
605. a. It was a miracle.
606. c. Through the gifts of God

PETER'S MINISTRY AND MIRACLES

607. b. While casting nets into the Sea of Galilee
608. c. The day of the Pentecost
609. b. The keys to the kingdom of heaven
610. b. John
611. a. Healing a man who had been lame from birth
612. a. Jesus forgives peter for denying him
613. b. Elijah and Moses
614. a. Of being responsible for the death of Jesus
615. d. That he would deny Jesus three times
616. a. Roman centurion
617. a. He bowed down before Peter.
618. b. That he was obeying God's will

619. a. By laying hands on him and praying
620. a. That it was accomplished through Jesus' name
621. c. Of being greedy and stealing money
622. b. To go out into all the world preaching
623. a. He speaks about God's message.
624. a. His incarceration and martyrdom
625. a. He was crucified upside down.

PAUL'S TRAVELS

626. a. Planting churches and spreading the gospel to Jews and Gentiles
627. d. Thirteen
628. a. Disciples who accompanied Paul on his journeys
629. b. Antioch
630. c. Corinth, Greece
631. d. Philippi
632. d. Romans
633. d. It was prophesied that he would be arrested by Gentiles.
634. a. Luke
635. a. Ananias of Damascus
636. d. Rome, Italy
637. c. Antioch
638. c. Paris
639. b. A leader of the Colossian Church
640. a. By boat
641. d. He had great success in converting Jews and Gentiles alike.
642. d. Koine Greek
643. a. Salvation through faith in Jesus Christ
644. b. Damascus
645. a. Paul
646. a. Thirteen (Scholars today debate on whether he wrote all thirteen himself.)
647. c. 46 CE
648. b. Asia Minor
649. a. They fled the city
650. b. Caesarea
651. b. Snake
652. b. He persecuted Christians
653. c. Nero
654. d. Rome

DISCIPLES

655. b. James the Greater
656. d. None
657. b. Matthias
658. a. That Matthew was a tax collector
659. a. "Do you love me more than these?"
660. d. All of the above
661. a. Two
662. a. James
663. d. John
664. b. Philip
665. b. Thomas
666. a. Fisherman
667. a. Peter
668. b. John
669. a. John the Baptist
670. a. Unknown
671. b. The disciples cast the lots
672. a. Paul
673. a. Non-Jewish believers
674. a. Cornelius
675. a. Stephen

676. c. He believed once he saw Jesus' wounds from the crucifixion
677. d. The Christian Church was established.
678. a. Jerusalem Council
679. b. Gentiles did not have to follow most of the Jewish rules.
680. c. Blasphemy
681. b. Doubting Thomas
682. a. Physician
683. b. Gentiles did not need to be circumcised.
684. c. Peter
685. a. The Great Commission

PERSECUTION OF THE EARLY CHRISTIANS

686. a. Martyrs
687. a. Nero
688. a. Acts of Apostles
689. c. Jewish Pharisees
690. d. Saul (Paul)
691. b. Burned at the stake and stabbed
692. a. They beat them.
693. c. Paganism
694. c. Burning of Rome
695. a. Public preaching
696. d. Diocletian
697. a. Refusal to worship Roman pagan gods
698. b. Rome
699. c. Edict of Milan
700. c. Death
701. a. Acts
702. b. Public sacrifice
703. a. Acts
704. c. Decius
705. a. Prayed
706. a. Banishment (B is also acceptable; Valerian would order the deaths of Christian leaders later in his reign.)
707. a. The early Roman Empire
708. b. Constantine I

EXPANSION OF THE GOSPEL

709. d. All of the above
710. a. Acts
711. b. The Great Commission
712. c. Luke
713. a. Philip
714. d. Matthew, Mark, Luke, and John
715. b. The Resurrection
716. d. Philip
717. d. All of the above
718. b. Luke and Acts
719. d. John Mark
720. b. Greek
721. c. The Word
722. d. Four
723. b. Matthew and Luke
724. b. Mark
725. a. Acts
726. d. John
727. b. Reinstation of Peter
728. c. Matthew
729. a. The Holy Spirit
730. a. Luke
731. c. Ethiopia

THE SECOND COMING OF JESUS

732. c. The Parousia
733. b. New Testament
734. a. Revelation
735. d. All of the above
736. a. Acts 1:10-11

737. d. All of the above
738. d. All of the above
739. a. Not to believe that Christ had already come again unless the rebellion had occurred
740. d. All of the above
741. a. Believers in him
742. a. It is not stated.
743. d. All three of them

THE MILLENIUM

744. b. Revelation
745. d. Forever
746. b. One thousand years
747. d. Chapter 20
748. a. Martyrs
749. b. All believers
750. b. They will suffer for their deeds.
751. d. Peace
752. d. They will live peacefully alongside humans.
753. d. Jesus' return
754. a. The resurrection of dead Christians and their rise to the skies
755. d. To restore God's kingdom on earth
756. c. Isaiah
757. a. He will be set free.
758. a. It will be purified.

FINAL JUDGMENT

759. d. All people
760. c. Good works done during life
761. b. Two
762. a. Sexual immorality
763. b. Unbelievers
764. b. Those whose names are not written in the Book of Life.
765. c. White
766. b. The second death
767. a. Jesus Christ
768. d. Through an examination of all they have said or done throughout their lifetime
769. c. Pagans
770. d. Chapter 20
771. d. Their punishment is everlasting.
772. b. Chapter 20

HEAVEN

773. a. Heaven
774. d. It is not specified.
775. a. John
776. d. The Great White Throne
777. a. They will experience no more sorrow.
778. d. Revelation
779. d. All of the above
780. b. Isaiah
781. b. No more suffering
782. a. Jasper
783. d. It is not specified.
784. d. You cannot marry in heaven.
785. c. Isaiah
786. d. Tree of life
787. c. Angels
788. a. Many different types of fruit
789. d. All of the above
790. a. Lapis
791. b. Revelation
792. b. Twelve

ANGELS

793. b. Two
794. It is never stated.
795. a. Lucifer
796. a. Archangel Gabriel
797. b. Revelation
798. b. Three (As a note, some traditions recognize more archangels.)
799. d. Israel
800. d. It is not specified.
801. b. Judges
802. c. Abaddon
803. d. Revelation
804. a. Two angels
805. a. Two
806. a. Genesis
807. c. Michael
808. c. "The Lord rebuke you!"
809. d. Abraham
810. c. Luke
811. d. It is not specified.
812. d. Genesis
813. a. Brought him food and drink
814. d. Joshua
815. c. Metatron
816. b. He was afraid.
817. c. Three (A is also acceptable.)
818. a. Cherubim

DEMONS

819. a. The pigs ran down a cliff into the sea.
820. a. Malicious disembodied human spirit
821. d. An elephant-like beast
822. d. There isn't a set belief for this.
823. a. Attack men
824. a. Incubus
825. d. A powerful fallen angel
826. "Go and tell the people what the Lord has done for you."
827. c. Evil spirits or demons
828. c. Seven
829. b. Satan
830. b. He helped her because of her faith.
831. c. The Seven Princes of Hell
832. d. None of the above
833. a. Cause sickness
834. b. "Come out of him!"
835. d. Satan

SATAN

836. d. All of the above
837. a. Genesis
838. a. Matthew
839. c. Armor of God
840. a. Chapter 1
841. b. By appealing to his hunger
842. c. The devil
843. a. Lucifer (Translations differ; some say "morning star.")
844. a. Adversary
845. a. James 4:7
846. c. A tempter
847. d. By being alert and of sober mind
848. b. Curse God (A is also acceptable, as some sources cite this as the translation.)
849. c. Satan
850. d. It is not specified.

If you enjoyed this book, a review on Amazon would be greatly appreciated because it would mean a lot to hear from you.

To leave a review:
1. Open your camera app.
2. Point your mobile device at the QR code.
3. The review page will appear in your web browser.

Thanks for your support!

Bible Trivia